SHOULD'VE SEEN THAT COMING

THAT COMING

Navigating the In-Between Moments of Acceptance, Surrender, and Resilience

JAMIE ESTELLE ROTH

LANDON
HAIL
PRESS

Paperback ISBN: 978-1-959955-51-1
Hardback ISBN: 978-1-959955-52-8

Cover design by Rich Johnson, Spectacle Photo
Published by Landon Hail Press

Dedicated to the loves of my life, Stewart, Mackenzie, Hayden, and Grady. And to those who do not feel seen, I see you, not only with my eyes, but with my heart and my soul

Close your eyes,
Fall in love
And stay there.

—Rumi

TABLE OF CONTENTS

FOREWORD

THIS YEAR, AT FORTY-FOUR, I found myself at a crossroads. I'd let go of employees, shifted my business, was considering moving my family, and for the first time in years, I was uncertain about the future and what I wanted. The questions of where I was headed and who I would become couldn't be quieted, or answered.

Was I merely navigating a midlife crisis or something far deeper—a dark night of the soul?

These are familiar questions when confronted with loss, whether through a diagnosis, the end of something cherished, or simply facing our own mortality as we age. While each of us will experience this journey of transformation differently, few of us will do it in literal darkness, as Jamie did.

In *Should've Seen That Coming,* Jamie shares a true story that is as heartbreaking as it is funny. Jamie brings us into her journey through adversity with vulnerability and honesty. Through her story, new understandings emerge:

- A deep appreciation of life's preciousness, with all its mixed emotions and experiences.

- The art of surrender—not as giving up, but as letting go.

- The power of living in the present and being in the moment.

- The importance of opening your mind and turning inward.

- How to find joy in the face of life's most terrifying uncertainties.

- And most importantly, how to seek and find the answers when no one else has them.

While all of us faced uncertainty during the global upheaval of 2020, grappling with challenges like depression, anxiety, and isolation, Jamie's journey took these struggles to an unimaginable level—one that, thankfully, few will ever have to endure. Her story is a testament to resilience, even in the darkest and most uncertain times.

I met Jamie eight years ago through her work as a real estate agent. Her humor, generosity, and authenticity made her stand out amongst hundreds of agents I'd worked with. This chance encounter led to a deep friendship, one that has profoundly impacted my life. Jamie has become an angel in my life, from helping me land a TEDx talk that transformed my career to guiding our family's move to Carmel.

When we reconnected in 2022, I was on my own journey of introspection. Her openness about her experiences inspired my own self-reflection. When Jamie asked me to be an early reader of her book, I was honored. I'd heard snippets of her journey over the years, but nothing prepared me for the impact of her story.

However this book found its way into your hands or ears, it will speak to you. Whether you're reading it for the first time or revisiting its pages, the wisdom in its pages will be a powerful guide.

Prepare to be opened up—to cry, to laugh, to rediscover that the answers we seek are often found in the wisdom we already hold. This book is a reminder that we are stronger, wiser, and more resourceful than we realize, and that there is a well of resilience within us waiting to be tapped.

Rebecca Cafiero, *Bestselling Author & Speaker*

INTRODUCTION

IF YOU'D TOLD ME THREE YEARS ago I would become a writer *because* I lost my vision, I would have laughed and wondered what you were smoking. I was fifty-one years old, and I had seen myself and the world the same way for half a century. What I am about to share with you is a journey into the greatest tsunami of change I've ever experienced. One minute I could see my children's faces. The next minute, I could not.

My story is not a story about a disability. It's not about being blind, because if you see the chapter names, we don't say the "B-word." This is a story about how a wild confluence of events gave me the ability to see myself, the world, and my life in an entirely new way. I'm not always sure I like what I see, but I know I am meant to see this way now. Ironic that I had to lose my vision, my old ways of seeing, to see the way I do now.

This new vision came with a price, but one I would pay again. Seeing things in a new light required one thing I wasn't too happy to accept at first: surrender. Why? Because I'm not a quitter, and that's what I used to think surrender meant. There is the word *end* in surrender. There is also *sur*, the Spanish word for south. To me, the word had always connoted things going south. Giving up. Throwing in the towel. Saying "fuck it" to the world. But if you look again at the letters in *surrender*, you can also find the words *nurse*, *sure*, and *render*.

In the course of thirty-six months, I would learn how to take care of my soul as much as I would learn how I had not taken care of it prior to my new way of seeing. I would become my own nurse. I would render deep change within my life to support a new reality. I would feel sure of my truth and my new path in life. None of it was easy, but it was all possible, and if you're in that liminal space, punching your fists into the face of surrender, I get it. I get you. And I hope my story offers comfort and companionship.

This is a story about how I learned how to surrender *without* despair. I know it sounds oxymoronic, which it is at first, especially if you're like me and believe you have to give up, give in, relinquish control. You do. But you don't. Not really. We'll get there. I promise.

First things first. I'm a straight shooter and always have been. So it might sound like bullshit if I tell you I'd been asking myself how to surrender without despair for three years. Because let's face it, at the beginning, I was despairing. I was depressed. I was losing hope as my vision continued to deteriorate. But one thing I wasn't losing was my spirit. She is badass and saved me from destroying myself with despair. She showed me there was another way to deal with the events in our lives that force us to surrender to what's next. Because I had a sneaking suspicion something big was happening for a reason.

The trick to it was learning how to surrender without losing my shit. My greatest fear was that if I surrendered, the despair of being in this situation for the rest of my life would make its home in my head and mess with the other parts of my psyche. I did not want to be depressed. I didn't want to give in to having no way out. I refused to settle for what I had been dealt without fighting to change it and make it better. This is how I thought about the dance with the devil between surrender and despair.

I was wrong. Surrender surprised me and came to mean something profound and beautiful. I realized I could let go of needing to be something and someone that no longer served me but gave me a false sense of happiness. I found a new Jamie in the in-between moments—those moments when your glance at your loved ones says everything without saying a word. When we feel connections we have with each other on a soul level. When we just know we are tethered to each other as we learn how to be present in our own lives. The moments where beauty surrounds us, seen and unseen—in nature, acts of kindness, watching our families grow, enjoying a good laugh with friends, or being the shoulder for someone to cry on. And I surrendered to a new way of living. Using my other senses to navigate through life and not having the ability to look at the expressions of others' faces has given me the gift of saying what is truly on my heart without the fear of being "seen" as a freak.

I learned how to surrender to my true self and the amazing new path I am walking, sharing my story, healing from the depths of my soul, releasing old hurts and traumas, and getting back to who I was born to be. I have come to believe surrender is a beautiful thread that, if you're willing to weave it into your life, allows you to let go of your ego and hold the hand of your spirit. I don't need my central vision to be led. I now allow my spirit to see for me and guide me to love and compassion. I have never been more present with myself. Surrender led me home.

My hope for those who read my story is that you learn to take the time to listen and be present with yourself. You will be shown a path to acceptance when you listen to your spirit while it lovingly reminds you that by navigating these many in-between moments, you will become aligned with your soul purpose. Being open to this sweet reality will show you that surrender is an act of letting go of what doesn't serve your higher good and will ultimately show you how damn resilient you can be in this life, allowing you to enjoy all that it has to offer. This lesson will help you through whatever life situation you're in so you don't get stuck in the shitty headspace found in self-preservation mode. I hope you learn that surrendering to any potentially challenging part of your life is not a bad thing but something that will help you grow even more in spite of the discomfort and pain. It's about the process of learning how to support yourself, escaping denial, and living in those in-between moments of your life, because those are the most beautiful moments we have.

CHAPTER 1

THE SPOT

UNTIL MONDAY, APRIL 12, 2021, I had vision like most people. I could see the world, the colors of the sky, the stretch marks on my belly, and the bags under my eyes—for better or worse—in vivid detail. I had never suffered any vision impairment, besides the expected consequences of aging, and for all intents and purposes had taken my vision for granted. It was a given. I had eyes. They did their job to help me navigate through life. When I went to bed, I expected to wake up the next morning and see myself and the world in all her glory and grotesqueness. This was the life I had always known—my vision showed me the way things were, but I had never questioned the way things *appeared* until the day I saw The Spot.

I was not sick. I had not been injured. None of my kids had figuratively punched me in the eye for telling them to clean their rooms. As far as I knew, all was good under the hood, as the saying goes. I'd had a pretty good night's sleep, considering I had just returned from helping our oldest son,Hayden, move back home early, due to COVID-19, from his first year at Colorado State University.

I can't lie. It was a stressful weekend. As much as I was excited to bring my son home again, I was dreading the hurricane in his room the morning we were to move. When we got there, I felt a gut punch seeing that nothing had been touched. There were no boxes packed, nothing marked or stacked or organized. My son has many skills and talents but sorely lacks the ability to clean his room on a regular basis. Just like in other kids' rooms, whose moms assured me I was not alone, piles of dirty clothes and leftover food in various containers littered the floor. Not a surface was free from clutter, not a shelf used for books. It was a hellish scene, especially for someone like me who appreciates the tidy side of life. We had two hours to pack up his shitstorm before the movers showed up. I turned on my inner drill sergeant and barked orders for him to get to work—pronto!—while I secretly nursed a massive hangover.

You can imagine the relief I felt returning to my controlled environment back home. While my son slept until noon the next morning, I was looking forward to my morning ritual—a cup of coffee and toast, alone. I skillfully put my contacts in and quietly exited the bedroom, making sure not to wake my husband, Stew, or the dog. I really wanted a morning of quiet reflection and the gift of no one asking me to do anything, fix anything, or drive anywhere for them. I settled down at my desk and opened my computer, drank my coffee, ate my toast, and watched the morning news, which I could do simultaneously *and* seamlessly like a magic trick. Multi-tasking was my middle name, my M.O., and the way I handled pretty much every task in my life, including the trick of scrolling through the latest Instagram posts while managing to blow dry my hair. These little tricks would soon become gifts I longed to have again. I didn't know an hourglass had been turned to take them away.

When I finally took a breath and focused on one thing, the morning news on the TV, I noticed there was something funky in the lower part of my left eye. A dark spot. For a second, I thought it might be a piece of eye gunk. Maybe I hadn't completely removed my mascara the night before? I rubbed it. The Spot didn't move. Or clear up. My vision was blurry. I tried again to rub my eye. Nothing cleared. The Spot remained. I stared at the TV screen to be sure it wasn't something on the display. Or maybe it was my residual hangover from a night of partying prior to helping my son move? I sat there a moment, perplexed, and shifted in my seat. I sipped my coffee. Closed my eyes. Blinked three times. I figured if I opened my eyes and The Spot disappeared, I'd shrug it off to lack of sleep and consider, maybe, taking a nap later that day. My wishful thinking didn't change the tenacity of The Spot, though. It was still there. And it wanted to stay.

I went to the bathroom to wash my eyes out with water but The Spot was still there. I turned off the water and stood there, feeling my heart pounding, knowing something was wrong but refusing to acknowledge it. Something deep in my gut was telling me it wasn't just eye gunk I could clear out with water or a concerted blink.

Normally, I would have freaked out and started thinking the worst, allowing anxiety and panic to rear their ugly heads. I tried another tactic—my tough act. Whenever I'd had this sense in my gut before, the uh-oh-oh-shit-this-might-be-bad feeling, I "masterfully" handled it by scoffing, tossing my hair, and repeating my daily mantra, "No worries, Jamie. Ain't nobody got time for that!" I had things to do. A family to care for. A college student to rehabilitate on the merits of tidy living. I had clients to serve, houses to sell. I didn't have time for The Spot.

All that said, my gut got louder over the course of the seconds that ticked by after all my attempts to remove The Spot had failed. By 7:30 a.m., I'd called my optometrist, Dr. Covert Gonzales, and left a message, hoping he would get back to me as soon as he got into the office. Covie, as we call him, was my older children's swim instructor before he became an optometrist. Now he has a young daughter who affectionately calls her dad Dr. Boctor, which is way more fun to say. Little did I know he would become a lifeline to my mental state by checking in with me via text and helping me get to other doctors to figure out what the hell this spot was all about.

I went about my morning and woke up our youngest, Grady, who was finishing up seventh grade. I looked forward to driving him to school, which was one of my favorite things to do with my kids. It was the only time I had my kids captive and could ask them so many questions that they had to talk to me. I'm not sure if they loved it as much as I did, but I cherished those conversations. Little did I know it would be one of the last times I would ever have the privilege of driving, let alone driving my child to school. The Spot was swooping in fast, like a thief, to clear me out, but not of the "gunk" in my eye.

Shortly after I woke Grady, my optometrist's office called me back, referred me to an ophthalmologist, and told me to contact them as soon as possible. I'm not a person who enjoys fire drills of any sort, so I refused to turn my attention to the smoke alarms going off in my head. I had too many other things to do than think about why the hell this spot was in my eye. I tried another tactic. I told myself it was a

13

rogue contact that loved my eye so much it didn't want to part from it. This story made sense, right?

I picked out my clothes and got dressed for work, as I had to meet with a client whose house I was selling. I had been a real estate agent for ten years and loved it. Being able to go into people's homes (legally) was awesome... but more awesome than that was helping my clients buy or sell a home so they could enjoy life's new adventures.

My appointment with the ophthalmologist was at 2 p.m. the day The Spot appeared. I was able to get there a little early to sit, wait, fill out paperwork, and people watch. I needed a distraction and people watching is great for that, especially when you are quietly panicking inside.

When my name was called to go back and meet with the doctor I was both excited and nervous. His assistant did the normal eye tests with me; one of those was reading the random letters on the opposing wall with one eye. I'd always prided myself on being able to read all of the letters, from large to small. I have to admit, though, I still had my contacts in so it made seeing those letters a little easier, despite The Spot in my left eye. I could at least see decently out of my right eye. I wasn't going to let The Spot hinder my vision test... yet.

The assistant to the doctor had me do a couple more tests on fancy equipment that took photos of the inside of the eye and the optic nerve. They had me take my contact lenses out and dilated my eyes, so the doctor could look at them a little better using the light and magnifying equipment. As I sat there waiting for the doctor to come in and explain to me why I had this spot in my eye, I honestly thought he was going to tell me I was a lazy contact wearer and had damaged my eyeball.

He finally walked into the room and although he was a very nice guy, he wasn't super warm and fuzzy. He took a few minutes to ask me what was going on with my vision. After explaining to him what I was seeing, he pulled the eye magnifier device toward my face and had me place my chin in the notch. The light this device uses to shine into your eye is sometimes unbearable, so keeping my eye open during this is always a challenge; this time was no exception. It feels like when that light is shone into your eye, the doctor is looking into your soul; it's a little unnerving.

After a few minutes of looking into both of my eyes, and probably my soul, too, the doctor pulled the device away from my face. Once my eyes acclimated to the lower light in the room, I was able to focus on his face. His expression was both nondescript and urgent. He said, "You are going to have to clear your schedule for the next couple days."

"So it wasn't a rogue contact?" I asked.

"No," he said. "You have inflammation in your optic nerve."

"That doesn't sound good," I said.

He basically laid out the possible causes and none of them were good. He said it could be anything from a brain tumor, cancer, multiple sclerosis, or optic neuritis to non-arterial ischemic optic neuropathy (NAION).

"You need to get an MRI so that we can really see what is going on."

I was stunned and felt like I left my body, which I would later learn is a common way for the spirit to cope with a traumatic moment through dissociation. I was somewhere floating in the room, hovering over myself, hearing his words. He asked if I had any questions. I did but couldn't pull them forward in my mind to ask because I was numb.

I left the office and drove home thinking my head was going to explode. *Did I have a tumor? Holy shit! What was happening to me?* I called my husband right away and as always, he talked me down and reassured me everything was going to be okay. My next call was to my sister, Sara, my go-to for so many things in my life, both good and bad. Being a medical transcriptionist, she immediately started looking up the possible diagnoses. I obviously knew the feasible outcomes of a brain tumor or MS diagnosis. Those without a doubt are life threatening and offered the ultimate fear factor. But when we researched the prognosis for optic neuritis, there was a possibility of temporary vision loss. With NAION, the ultimate and totally terrifying potential reality was blindness. I could feel her fear, panic, and urgency through the phone, so, although I felt the same, I did my best to make jokes and laugh about it because thinking about what the doctor said was too much for my mind and body to handle. We decided we would both take a breath and wait to see the MRI results before we, or really I, completely lost my shit!

I had to wait a week before the insurance company approved my MRI. Insurance is such a blessing and a curse because you are essentially at the insurance company's mercy as to when and where you get treatment for any ailments you may have. In the big scheme of things you wouldn't think a week was a long time, but it was for me, since The Spot had grown from the size of a corn kernel in my lower left eye to the size of an almond. It was basically filling up half of my visual field with darkness.

I was super anxious the morning I went in for my MRI. It wasn't my first time in the tube as I'd had to get an MRI a few years prior for my ankle. But let's be honest, although science is amazing and laying in a metal tube (that feels more like a coffin) can take pictures of your insides to help find any bad invaders, it is one of the more disturbing life experiences to endure. This time, my whole body was put into the open-ended tube and they made me as comfortable as possible, placed a warm blanket over me, stuck an IV in my arm for a contrast dye to be shot into my body to help find any impurities, and, the cherry on top of it all, placed a mesh mask over my face to inhibit me from moving my head too much. They also gave me a "get me the hell out of here" button to push if I started to get too anxious.

I laid in the MRI tube for almost forty-five minutes. It was the longest forty-five minutes of my life, so when I survived it, I thought, *Praise the Lord!* I left the hospital thrilled to be done but apprehensive about what the MRI would reveal.

The next few days were excruciating waiting for the doctor to call me with the results. The waiting became a space for me to freefall into the denial that anything was actually wrong. During that week, I went about my life like normal, attending my kids' sporting events and tending to my work obligations as if I wasn't awaiting impending death or blindness. All the while, I alone was forced to deal with the pit of fear and helplessness in my stomach. When the MRI doctor's office finally did call me, they asked me to come in so the doctor could go over the MRI results with me in person. Well, that sounded ominous.

Unfortunately, the first available appointment was a week later. The waiting was killing me. I would wake up each morning afraid I was going to face complete darkness in both eyes. I would say a prayer asking for vision every morning before I opened my eyes and an answer as to why

17

the hell this was happening to me. I was so frustrated with having to constantly advocate for myself in the face of doctors who didn't have any straightforward answers. Being in this constant, jacked-up limbo made it hard to maintain my genuine positivity. The effort for all of it was so damn exhausting.

When I finally got back in to see the doctor, my left eye was almost three-fourths full of darkness. The Spot had grown. He told me the MRI showed inflammation of my optic nerve but that was about it. Thank God, there was no sign of cancer, a tumor, or MS. The other two options, as the other doctor had told me, were optic neuritis or NAION. Those words sounded so foreign to me, and I felt as if I stepped out of my head for a moment when he was explaining it all because it was too much to comprehend.

I wished I had brought my husband with me so he could hear and process everything the doctor was saying and explain it in layman's terms, making it easier for me to comprehend what was happening to me. I checked back into my mind just as the doctor was telling me he was going to refer me to a retina specialist in their office. I agreed to whatever and whoever he thought would be able to help me; I was all in and would see any specialist at this point.

By the time I met with the retina specialist, it was the first week of May, about a month since seeing The Spot for the first time. He had me go through the same tests the other doctor had done, but by this time the vision in my left eye was completely dark. It was like a bucket of dirty water had filled my eye; I couldn't see any light whatsoever.

I tried to calm myself down when the eye went completely dark. I would tell myself that my new nickname would be "One-Eyed Jack" and that I should get that tattooed somewhere on my body. Thank goodness my right eye was still as clear as ever and I could still drive myself, read my emails and texts, and pretend everything was just fine. *Lots of people live normal lives with the use of just one eye, right?*

Once the tests were done and the retina specialist finished shining the bright light into my eyes, he sat back in his stool and said to me with the most sympathetic look and voice, "I am so sorry, but there is nothing I can do for you." Translation: *"You are screwed!"*

All of the build-up to this moment—The Spot continuing to engulf my left eye and the agonizing waiting game—were thwarted by this sweet doctor who wasn't able to fix me. He couldn't give me any answers, even though I learned my macula and retina, as well as my optic nerve, were inflamed. A trifecta of eye inflammation. It was like my eye was shutting down—she was tired and over this shit—but beyond that, no definite diagnosis.

I could feel the doctor's sadness because there was nothing he could do to help me. Processing my non-diagnosis and his humanity at the same time led me to my go-to *modus operandi*. I have this weird habit of making sure everyone is okay and not sad; I call it a positive attitude. My response to him was, "It's okay, we will figure this out. I will be okay, don't worry about me."

I think he was a little taken aback at my response. I was in denial and refused to wilt like a flower. He suggested I see a neuro-ophthalmologist and said he would give me a referral to Stanford Eye Center or to a local neurologist who specializes in ophthalmology. I wasn't going to be able to get an appointment with Stanford for another two weeks, so I opted for going to see the local neurologist instead.

About a week and a half later, I met with the neurologist who specializes in ophthalmology. After a two-hour appointment with him and a slip to get blood work done to rule out a bacterial infection, I was scheduled to see him in another week to go over the results and treatment plan. At this point, a voice screamed within my body, "Where the hell is the urgency!?" I had been existing in a space of fear and frustration for two months, screaming for anybody to hear or see me, and no one was listening. Every professional who couldn't figure me out just handed me off to the next doctor. It was normal to feel like I was shouting helplessly into the void. But due to my desire for everything to be okay, aka to be in control, I told myself One-Eyed Jack would be just fine.

My follow-up appointment was in the first week of May; my husband was traveling to Denver to help our daughter, Mackenzie, move home for the summer that same week. My two boys were home due to COVID-19 restrictions and my husband traveled often, so I didn't worry too much about it. Both boys were finishing up school; my older son was able to take his classes online to finish his year, while my younger son's school was allowing the kids back on campus with restrictions. But he didn't care about any of that—he was just happy to be back with his friends. Although he is a really good kid and a good student, he was playing a lot of video games during the lockdown. He had started to think he was going to be a professional gamer, and who needs school for that, anyway? So, when his school said they were going to have the kids return to the actual classroom, I was beyond excited.

It may sound like my family was simply going about life as usual. They were very supportive in everything I would share with them about my condition, but as moms do, I downplayed the severity of my medical situation. The last thing I wanted was for them to feel my fear and anxiety. Plus, as everyone knows, when Mom goes down, it's like the wi-fi signal in the house has vanished. I didn't want to put anybody out, and I wanted to go about my life like nothing was wrong. I was in denial with a capital D, and because of that, my husband and children were totally oblivious to the life-changing impact of my condition.

I met with the doctor toward the end of the week to go over my blood work and find out why the hell my eye was dark, why this had happened to me, and how to fix it. I had my older son go with me so I could have him there to help me understand what the doctor said, because as you know, sometimes when the doctors go over the results of any tests, they talk to you like you are a third-year resident in medical school. I always have to go back and read the notes to really absorb what they have told me. This time I made sure to pay attention, but I realized the blood tests were a disappointment. The phlebotomist took about fifteen vials of blood from me and when the doctor looked at the results, he looked annoyed. He had checked me for bacterial infections ranging from Rocky Mountain Fever to rat poop bacteria, dog poop bacteria to tuberculosis. All of the blood work came back negative. I had none of these.

I asked, "What do we do now?" He said the standard treatment for inflammation, whether in the body or optic nerve, is corticosteroids. The dosages of the steroids are what differ when it comes to treatment of the above-mentioned conditions. For treatment of the optic nerve and to get the inflammation down, he prescribed 1000 milligrams of corticosteroids, by mouth, per day, for three days. So, that is exactly what I did. I picked up my prescription from the pharmacy and proceeded to take 1000 milligrams of corticosteroids by mouth for the next three days. I took the first dose on a Friday, and I totally get why some people take steroids. I felt like this must be what it feels like to be on cocaine, just safer. Right? Either way, I had a ton of energy and got a lot of stuff done in my house. The bathrooms were organized, I cleaned my entire house in record time, I organized my pantry, and I tried to stay as calm as possible. I took fairly brisk walks every day to burn off some of the energy, and when I talked with friends I would see along my walk, the pissed-off version of me came through and I sounded like "Rowdy" Roddy Piper the WWE wrestler getting ready for a championship wrestling match. I felt like I could run for miles, lift a car at the end of my run, and still have the energy to cook dinner. I also felt out of control at the same time.

With my one good eye, I was still able to read my computer and went down the rabbit hole of researching what "roids" could do to someone who takes a dosage as high as mine. I kept imagining myself looking like a Cabbage Patch Doll at the end of the three days due to the fact that steroids can cause a person to retain fluids. The roids were already taking their toll. With one good eye, I could see that my face and body were puffing up like pastry dough.

The following Monday, I sat down at a table in my office to work on a painting I had begun before The Spot showed up in my life. Let's be clear, I am not an artist and the painting was a Paint by Numbers. While I was not intending to become Michelangelo, there was something about working on this type of painting that calmed my mind, and God knows, I needed that. I had one fully functioning eye and was pretty confident I could see the small numbers to paint. However, it was harder to focus on the lines I had to paint between those numbers. What should have been a relaxing project quickly morphed into something frustrating and sad. So I stopped and put the paints away.

It was a really strange and jacked-up weekend of "roids," anxiety, and being afraid I would freak the fuck out on anyone who came within five feet of me. Needless to say, I was glad when the three-day regimen of taking the steroids ended—only to meet with a worse fate.

CHAPTER 2

SPARKLES & IZODS

I WAS EXPECTING A CALL from my doctor to check on me after my harrowing weekend of roid rage. Eventually, his receptionist called, but not the doctor. I couldn't believe it. There was no urgency, and I was pissed. By now it was the beginning of the last week in May, and none of the treatments had done anything to fix The Spot. I contacted Stanford that same day and made an appointment with a neuro-ophthalmologist and was fortunate to get in on June 1. I needed help. Something else was brewing. Like the nuanced line between the spaces in my painting, I was experiencing severe pain in the lower left quadrant of my belly. It initially felt like really bad cramps, but I knew it had nothing to do with menstruation. I'd had my uterus taken out the year before, and not just because I wanted to wear white pants anytime I wanted. My girly parts were getting attacked by fibroids and polyps and they caused intense pain when I had my period each month. The pain I was experiencing then was similar to super painful menstrual cramps, like what I was currently feeling. I also thought I was having breakthrough bleeding, which I knew was impossible without a uterus.

Something was very wrong and nothing was making sense.

I contacted my gynecologist and he said he wanted me to treat whatever might be going on in my gut. His recommendation was to take a general antibiotic. Being a "good patient," I picked up the prescription from the pharmacy and immediately started taking the antibiotics without questioning his order. They weren't working the way I had hoped. The pain in my gut didn't subside and actually became worse. I didn't have time or energy for this; I just wanted The Spot to go away, the pain to end, and my life to return to "normal."

Thankfully, Stew and Mackenzie were home from their travels in Denver to help me navigate this conundrum. I was definitely in denial. We had just been through this scenario only a few months prior when I had been diagnosed with diverticulitis. Fun fact: I didn't even know what the hell diverticulitis was but I did know it hurt like a mother-f'er.

My husband took me to the hospital where we waited patiently in the ER. The ER doctor did a CT scan on me that showed another confirmed diverticulitis diagnosis. Similar to the last crisis, the ER doc prescribed yet another antibiotic and said that diverticulitis is associated with bacteria and other nasty things getting stuck in little bubbles in the colon that can become infected and cause inflammation. If not treated, the condition can become very serious and sometimes life-threatening.

With this cheerful information, I asked the ER doc, "What do I eat then? Is there a specific diet that I should follow so that this doesn't happen again?"

He stared at me flatly and said, "I am not quite sure—why don't you Google it."

I looked at Stew with my good eye. He locked eyes with me and we both exchanged a WTF look. He drove me home where I sat down at my computer and Googled my question. Thanks, doctor. I found all kinds of information and decided to go with the BRAT diet (bananas, rice, apples, and toast). I could also eat pasta and any food without fiber or protein. I was on a high-carb diet and could only imagine how I'd balloon. On the flip side of that, who doesn't want to just eat carbs? As much as I wasn't thrilled to abide by this new "diet," at least I understood what was happening during the second flare-up. Little did I know, though, what I should have been eating was a clear liquid diet, as that is the best way to help the digestive system heal while in a diverticulitis flare-up. I also knew I didn't want to go back to the ER, but the pain continued getting worse. I couldn't wait to see my doctor because the intensity gradually got so bad I couldn't even stand up straight. I looked like the Hunchback of Notre Dame, minus the hunch but with a painful grimace on my face.

I was beside myself with anger, sadness, and pain. My intuition was telling me the steroids I had taken the week before had triggered this second flare-up, and I was so glad I chose not to continue seeing Dr. Roids, who prescribed the steroids.

A week later on June 1, Stew drove me to the Stanford Eye Center for my appointment, even though I wanted to drive myself. We both knew that was ludicrous. I needed Stew to be my eyes on the road, my hands on the wheel, my foot on the gas. I hated that I was slowly giving up my privilege of driving, but by that point, no stubbornness could convince even me that I could drive myself to Palo Alto. I also needed Stew's eyes and ears to help me absorb whatever they were going to tell me about what was happening to my eye and the dark spot that was still there.

Once we signed in at the front desk it was only a short time before my name was called. I underwent another sequence of eye tests, photos of my eye (inside and outside), and photos of my optic nerve. Those tests and photos took about thirty to forty-five minutes, during which I had to keep my eyes open wide and stare at a dot, not blinking once during the procedure. I did my best to keep a straight face and cooperate with the technician, but while I waited for the neuro-ophthalmologist to come into the exam room, hoping for good news, I had a yucky feeling in my gut I chose to ignore.

When the doctor finally came into the room, she had a welcoming smile on her face. I was certain she was going to tell me all was good. I expected her to give me some eye drops and tell me my cloudy vision would clear up and the darkness would be gone forever. My fantasy ended when she started to speak.

"So, your left eye is done. Now we have to work on saving your right eye."

Wait. What did she say? *My left eye is done?* What is *done* in this situation? Done like for today? Or doomed forever? Are we talking "the damn spot will be there for the rest of my life" done? And what did she mean about saving my right eye? Righty was my trusted eye. It helped me ace the vision tests and see all those little letters, with contacts. Righty would help me finish my Paint by Numbers masterpiece and restore my sense of sanity and serenity.

I did not like hearing the word *done*. I was not done. My eyes were not done. I wasn't a quitter. I wasn't the kind of person who easily gave up a fight. The only thing I was done with was hearing her voice, her news, and the cavalier tone with which she delivered it.

The look on my face must have revealed exactly what I was thinking, which was, excuse my French, *What in the mother-fucking love of God are you saying?*

She explained she wanted to do a few more tests the following week in order to support her prognosis, and then she would have a better treatment regimen. These tests included injecting an IV contrast into my veins, which would display any possible leakage in the vessels of my eyes. This would ultimately confirm her suspicions that the leakage from the vessels in my eyes was drowning my optic nerve. It felt like I was drop-kicked in the stomach and I left the clinic feeling like Flat Jamie—a cardboard cutout that nobody, I assumed, would want to take their picture with or hug.

The two-hour drive home was mostly quiet as Stew and I processed what she had just said to us. I honestly thought I was living in an alternate universe and was still in denial.

The following Tuesday, I went out to dinner with some girlfriends and my daughter. While we were enjoying our evening, I received a phone call from my neuro-ophthalmologist. She proceeded to tell me the tests we had done the day before showed some inflammation and leakage in the vessels of my eyes and because of that she was able to get me admitted to Stanford Hospital where I would have more blood work done, get another MRI, and have a lumbar puncture done as well. When I heard her say this I thought I was going to pass out, vomit, and run down the street screaming in fear—all at the same time. It was surreal. I was so grateful my daughter was with me. The doctor wanted me at the hospital that next day. This is when shit got real; there was finally a sense of urgency.

I spent the next four days at Stanford Hospital. They did all of the tests and blood work and the results were all normal. There was still inflammation in my optic nerve but nothing else to write home about. The one worry I had, besides my vision leaving me in the dark, was that I would get another flare-up of diverticulitis. The doctors told me I was on an antibiotic that would help with that so a flare-up shouldn't happen after my stay at the hospital. I assumed it was the same antibiotic I had been prescribed for my previous diverticulitis flare-up, so I was beside myself with hope when I was given the green light to go home.

On the day I was to be discharged, one of the attending doctors asked me if my vision had changed at all in my right eye. Up until that day, my right eye was perfect and I didn't have any issues with a spot showing up and making that eye dark, but there was something different that day. I didn't want to tell the doctor because I thought she would make me stay another day, but my gut told me to speak up or forever hold my peace. I reluctantly confessed to her what I was seeing. Although I had no ominous dark spot in my right eye, I instead saw sparkles and an IZOD (as in the little alligator from those polo shirts) floating around in my eye. I was not high, drunk, or sedated. She looked at me like I was an alien when I mentioned the IZOD. I forgot that anyone under forty-five years old might not remember how awesome and cool IZOD polos were to wear in the '80s. Regardless of her comprehension of what was in my field of vision, I knew the sense of urgency for my medical well-being had dwindled when she didn't push for me to stay longer after this revelation.

This underscored the feeling that there were so many eyes looking at me yet I wasn't being seen. During my time in the hospital, I stayed on the neurology floor, which was funny for many reasons, including the fact that staff communicated via sticky notes on my door to inform one another I'd simply had my eyes dilated, not the typical indication of a stroke. Being that it's a teaching hospital, I never saw my neuro-ophthalmologist while I was there. Instead I was seen by resident neuro-ophthalmologists who couldn't really answer my questions as to why this was happening and how to heal me.

When I was finally released from the hospital I was a master at pushing down my fear, anxiety, and acknowledgement of what was potentially happening with my eyesight. I wanted to get back to my family and life to pretend everything was fine, the IZOD would disappear, and the sparkles would fade.

Stew had reached out to my sister before I went to Stanford and asked her to come down and stay with the kids and the dog while I was in the hospital. I found out later that Stew called Sara and said to her, "You might want to come down sooner rather than later because I don't know if Jamie will be able to see you. We don't know what is going to happen with her vision." It was so nice to have my sister there, along with all three of my kiddos.

I had been home for about three days when shit got real. I was up in the morning on June 14, which was also my husband's birthday, and was working with a client to put together an offer on a property. I had been on the phone with the listing agent and was thankfully able to negotiate the terms of the offer and get my client into escrow on the house.

All the while, I was in pretty significant pain in my lower abdominal area again. I knew exactly what was going on and told myself I could just rest and it would subside and get better on its own. But when I couldn't sit up and had to roll onto my stomach and slither off the bed to walk, looking again like the Hunchback of Notre Dame, I knew it was bad.

After taking another Percocet later that evening with no relief, I had to face the truth and go to the hospital. I did not want to go, but when my sister and husband both insisted, I had no choice. They called an ambulance, and being that my husband was a retired firefighter, the medic and three firefighters who showed up knew me and Stew. While some women fantasize about an army of firefighters showing up to rescue them, all I felt was deep embarrassment. It didn't feel like an emergency, not the kind that would merit four hulking men to get me out of bed. One of the worst parts of that transition from bed to gurney was when I looked at Grady, who had big crocodile tears in his eyes. I told myself I had to keep it together for him and everybody else in my family.

At the local hospital, the pain in my abdominal area was ten times worse than it was at my house just a few minutes prior. Maybe it grew more acute because I knew I could get help and finally allowed myself to feel it versus hide it. When I arrived at the ER, I was asked the standard "What is your pain level?" question. They pointed to a chart that represented levels ranging from zero to ten. I strained to see it with my one good eye through the agony. Pain at the lowest end of the scale was represented by a happy, green smiling emoji; the "worst pain you've ever felt in your life" was represented by what looked like an inconsolable red-faced crying emoji. I was at an eight, which translated to an orange, depressed-looking sad-face emoji. I would compare the severity of what I was feeling to the last stages of labor but with no epidural and nothing beautiful at the finish line to hold in my arms as a reward for the struggle. After I communicated my level-eight sadness and physical inner torture, I was wheeled into a room and given a dose of morphine to help with the pain. It worked for a minute. They subsequently gave me three more doses to help, but the morphine barely touched it.

Shortly after my last dose of morphine, the ER doctor arrived and suggested giving me a stronger painkiller, which was Dilaudid. When the nurse came in to administer it, I was momentarily frozen when he asked my husband, who was scrolling a news feed on his phone, to monitor me and make sure I was still breathing. Apparently Dilaudid is so intense it has the potential to interfere with respiratory function. *Holy mother of God,* I thought. *Is this really happening?* My wonderful husband tried valiantly to remind me to breathe, but little did I know he was also holding his breath because he was overwhelmed by the very real scenario in which I could die. Unbeknownst to me at this time, I had gone into sepsis, and my body was quickly crashing. I *was* dying. Due to Stew's first responder training and experience, he was fully aware of the gravity of this situation. They subsequently gave me a second dose of Dilaudid and thankfully the nurse then put a nasal cannula on me so neither Stew nor I had to worry about whether I was about to take my last breath—at least for the time being.

Meanwhile, my situation perplexed everyone, and soon other doctors and nurses started to come into my room with the same questions. "What's going on with your eyes?" "How is your vision now?" "Did Stanford find out what was causing your vision loss?" I responded to each of them with the same answer: "I don't know!"

At some point during the night, I underwent a CT scan to see what the hell was going on with my gut. Finally, the surgeon on call arrived with the results. "Your CT scan shows that you have a perforated colon and we will most likely have to do surgery to repair it and as a result, you could have a colostomy bag for the next three to six months." The diverticulitis had reared its ugly head again, but this time it was coming in for the kill.

I glanced over at Stew, who was holding on by a thread. I was numb and sobbed. This was my worst nightmare. Not only might I lose my sight but I would have a shit bag attached to my body. I wanted everyone to tell me this was all a joke. That none of this was real and that the entire sequence of events was a bad trip after my "girls gone wild" weekend in Denver. I kept asking myself, "How the hell did this all happen to me?" Two months ago I was living my best life.

I had no idea my best life was yet to come.

But I had a major bridge to cross first.

CHAPTER 3

AN IRISH GOODBYE

LYING IN THE EMERGENCY ROOM hospital bed, swimming in a mixture of avoidance and acceptance regarding the real and imminent possibility of surgery and a colostomy bag, memories flooded back to the weekend before The Spot reared its ugly head.

I was so excited because I had just received my second dose of the COVID-19 vaccine and felt safe, especially because I was flying to Colorado with my friend Kristen to help our sons move from their freshman dorms at Fort Collins. I was also going to see Mackenzie, who was joining me and Kristen the night prior to the move. It was the first time Kristen and I had traveled together, and I was looking forward to girl time before we encountered the unknown abyss of a male college dorm on moving day.

We were staying at a bougie hotel in Denver and met Mackenzie in the hotel bar before going to dinner. I was brimming with energy, feeling so happy to be in the midst of other people and out of the house in some kind of public space after the pandemic. I was an extrovert. I needed other energy to fill me up. I craved it and was ready to grab it in any way I could. I swear, I stood in the hotel lobby and sniffed the air for my hit of extroversion.

Inadvertently, I invited my alter ego to show up that night, too. She was ready to have a good time, and nothing was going to stop her. We had a few drinks at the bar before dinner and a few more at dinner. We were enjoying a great night, talking, laughing and just having fun. We ended up back at the hotel bar that had a patio with outdoor fire pits.

We snagged some seats outside and enjoyed another cocktail and more laughs and conversation around the firepit. I had the perfect buzz and was so happy and content. A few drinks in, we noticed an older gentleman sitting in one of the chairs at our fire pit. He seemed like a nice guy; he was probably in his seventies and was as buzzed as we were. He was trying to make conversation with us and I was ignoring him as much as possible, solely because I didn't have the energy to have a conversation with a random guy.

The next moment, I overheard Mackenzie talking to another older guy and wondered if we had checked into an old folks hotel. This other older man seemed nice, too, and I heard him ask Mackenzie, "Do you want this joint?" He had a beautiful Irish accent; it turned out he and his buddy were from Ireland. They finally won my attention and that's when twenty-two-year-old Jamie showed up. I was not a mom at that moment. I said to the Irish man, "Yes, we will take that joint," then turned to my daughter and said, "Light it up, babe!"

Mackenzie stared at me, drop-jawed. I smiled and shrugged and beckoned her to pass the joint. Did I make a good decision? Absolutely not, and everything began to go wrong after that. We teach our children not to take drugs from strangers, yet here I was encouraging my kid to light up a joint from a random Irishman. My amazing daughter did not take the joint, but I did. And thank God it wasn't laced with anything. It was a perfect joint, and I laughed my ass off.

At one point, I was laughing so hard I thought my eyes were going to pop out of my head. I hadn't laughed that hard in a long time. What I didn't know at the time is that I likely popped a blood vessel, which may have started my saga. I woke up the next morning with a hangover that lasted the entire weekend, but I remembered the evening of fun, laughs, and Irish weed. I got back into mom mode, tucking my twenty-two-year-old self into memory and whispering, "Next time you show up, can you make some better choices?"

Trying to clear out my son's dorm room the next day was no easy task. Meanwhile, we were a mile high in elevation, the air was bone dry, and I was dehydrated. The perfect storm was brewing. I would later learn that if the optic nerves in the eyes are deprived of oxygen for even a small amount of time, they will shut down—and possibly result in permanent vision impairment. I had no idea the flight back at 33,000 feet would contribute to the inflammation, dehydration, and ensuing shitshow that landed me in the hospital.

Back in the ER, I was finally admitted to a hospital room and received the miraculous gift of another surgeon, Dr. Mark Vierra, who looked at my chart and suggested an alternate solution for my perforated colon. He inserted a drain to allow my broken bowel to heal. He explained the drain would take the yuck out, so I could wait to have surgery. Given the circumstances, I was elated to hear the news. Despite the discomfort of needing this drainage tube, it was ironically a godsend as it teamed up with a strong round of antibiotics to stave off the sepsis that was threatening to land the final blow.

With the drain in my gut now plugging the hole in my colon, I was placed into a room in the surgical unit. By this time it was June 15. I felt good, of course, with oxy and morphine easing the pain. I remember taking a call with my friend Kristen, the gal who traveled to Denver with me that fateful weekend. We were reminiscing about our younger alter egos indulging in pot and a lot of brown liquor like we were at our first frat party. She recounted the old man offering us one more temptation—a mound of blow off his AARP card, a detail we could not forget. We weren't interested in the bump and said no thanks, but remembering this moment made me laugh so hard I snorted, howled, and then did something very unexpected and horrifying. I thought I peed in my bed and when I looked down, I saw it wasn't actually pee but poop. It turns out that every time I laughed, I also queefed. As I confessed this to Kristen, she was cracking up but also concerned, as I continued to explain to her that not only did I have a perforated colon but I also had a vaginal fistula. You can't make this shit up. Literally. It was happening to me.

You would think I would have folded and cried with sorrow for days, but for some unknown reason, I had a sense of humor through it all and that saved my sanity. There were days when I broke down and entertained a pity party. But humor would save me and help me cope with the scary situation, as I was waiting in the hospital to find out what they were going to do about my colon, while my right eye and its vision had changed.

When the doctors or nurses asked what I was experiencing with my right eye, aka Righty, I told them it was like a shade being drawn over the top of my visual field. If I tried to look at anyone, I couldn't see above their forehead. Other than that, my right eye had perfect vision. Since this was happening during COVID-19 protocols, everyone in the hospital was masked to prevent the spread of the virus. None of us were seeing each other clearly. Meanwhile, several other doctors and nurses, who were not assigned to me, stopped by my room to ask about my vision. I had suddenly become a curiosity, like a circus freak show, queefing on demand with impaired vision. It was comedic. And cruel. And complicated.

By June 17, the neurologist, Dr. Roids, who I had met in May, also stopped by for a visit and checked on my vision. He was there for over an hour. After doing a few rudimentary tests, he bluntly delivered the news, "Here is the deal, Jamie, we can't help you here. You need to go back up to Stanford." He explained they possessed the technology and means to help me, not only with my gut but with my eyesight. It did make sense considering my team of eye doctors and medical records were already established there.

He said they had admitted me to Stanford but were waiting to hear when a bed would be available. Then he added, "It looks like they have a waitlist of about twenty people, so it could be later tonight that you are transported up there or it could be a few days."

A few days. Stuck in that hospitable bed. I hoped Kristen would call back. I needed to laugh my way through this, but our one memory was not going to carry me all the way through. Little did I know, behind the scenes of my sordid life drama, Stew was taking the lead and communicating with all of my friends and family. It still makes me smile with pride, thinking about him staying on top of this intense communication between his own friends and nearly a dozen other chat groups of our mutual friends and family going on simultaneously. My college friends composed one of those groups, and I will be forever grateful to those women. One of my college roommates, Katie, immediately called Stew to get more details about my condition. When she learned I needed to transfer to Stanford Hospital, she remembered another one of our college roommates, Lynette, worked there. The irony is Lynette and I hadn't been in touch for more than a decade, but as I was starting to learn, the Universe works in mysterious ways.

When Katie told her what was happening, Lynette made some calls and secured a bed for me within an hour at Stanford. To this day, I still get chills and tears fill my eyes when I think about this. I was realizing the connections we make in life can be more important than we realize. My angels were watching over me and knew how to not only get me the help I needed but also reconnect me with these women from my early twenties, who knew my alter ego (the twenty-two--year-old me) so well.

I made it up to Stanford late on the night of June 17 and stayed for five days, having daily visits from a team of neurologists, ophthalmologists, and surgeons. The neurologists all asked the same question, "How many fingers am I holding up?" The ophthalmologists visited every evening with a mobile eye-looking glass device that shone light into my eye for long periods of time. When the surgeons came, I was suddenly smitten. Of course, Stanford had to have the most gorgeous looking doctors checking on my drain and stretch-marked belly. I tried to distract them with the story of the Irish weed, wondering if that might have caused my vision issue, but they all agreed the pot could have only helped, as it is a natural anti-inflammatory.

No consensus had been reached on the surgery for my colon, so they kept me on a diet of clear liquids consisting of broth, a popsicle, some jello, and juice. After being on this type of diet for a little over a week, I concluded this was the most expensive weight-loss camp I could ever attend. When one of the doctors asked if there was anything I needed, I emphatically ordered, "Yes, first I want you to fix my eyesight! Besides that, I'd like a crispy carne asada taco and a Negro Modelo… that's what I want."

By June 21, my team of doctors at Stanford had run every test imaginable, including multiple MRIs, blood draws, and a PET scan, without any understanding of why my eyesight was jacked up. Every time the doctors and nurses would come in to talk or help me, all I could think to myself was, *Why are they helping me? They don't have to do this.* My logical brain said, *Bitch, they get paid to do this! This is their job!* But the unworthy side of my brain couldn't help but wonder, *Why me? I'm just Jamie. Why would they want to help me?* These dark reflections created a rabbit hole of feeling like not enough. The heaviness of this unworthiness sat with me like an elephant on my chest.

That night, I found myself sitting on a hospital toilet with very limited visits from family and friends. COVID-19 protocols were still in place, and I was two hours from home, feeling stuck and despairing. Nobody had any answers to what was happening to me or why. My vision was getting worse. My hope was fading.

It was the first time I started to ask dark questions, which scared me because I had always thought of myself as an optimistic person. Now, however, I began to seriously consider the option that seemed like it might be a nice way to escape my pain. *Would dying free me? If I quietly passed away in the night, everyone would be okay, right?* It was an honest question. Not exactly suicidal, but it was the first time I actually felt so defeated that death seemed like a more viable option than this constant state of fear and self-loathing that had swallowed me up. I didn't want my situation to be a burden on anyone else, either, and yet I felt the palpable strain of this situation on my whole family.

But par for the course, my tenacious spirit was one that no disability would destroy, and I quickly snapped out of my dark thoughts. I got up from the cold hospital toilet and started a long hard conversation with myself. I had to find a way through the present sludge without contaminating myself or anyone else.

Before digging deep, however, I needed to release a little frustration. In the past, masturbation had always been an option, but with my new party favor attached to my gut and the double IVs in my arms, I was terrified of getting tangled up and setting off an alarm on the many devices attached to me with sticky tape and wires. There would be no way to release myself with a simple orgasm, so I opted to scream instead and hurled a deep, guttural howl into the bleached hospital pillow. When that was done, I took a deep breath. My throat felt sore. My body buzzed from adrenaline. I sat back in my bed and asked myself, *How the hell did I get here?*

I faced a choice. I could either rise to the occasion or destroy myself with these dark thoughts and death wishes. It was time for me to change my thoughts—put on my big-girl panties and nut the fuck up. I had to keep fighting for myself and my family. I wanted to see my children. I was determined to be at the most important moments of their lives—graduations, weddings, the birth of their children—despite my eyes. But even more importantly, I wanted to be there for the small moments, the in-between moments of their lives, and mine, too.

The doctors finally discharged me on June 22. I still had my super sweet vaginal fistula and "party favor" drain attached to my damaged colon, as it needed time to heal before I could be a candidate for surgery. In the doctor's words, if they tried to operate at this time, it would look something like trying to stitch together jello. Needless to say, I still didn't have any answers for my eyesight disappearing, but at that point I didn't care. I was beyond excited to go home. I wanted to hug my kids and husband and reassure them I was going to be okay. I couldn't wait to see my children's faces. I knew something was going to happen to my eyesight and I might not be able to see their faces clearly for much longer.

Just before I was discharged, I shared a moment with the lead surgeon and broke down in front of her and my daughter, who was visiting.

"Jamie, is everything okay?" she asked, a bit frozen in the doorway, seeing me choking back the tears. I glanced at my daughter.

"I'm scared…" I said.

The surgeon nodded. "I understand. It's natural to feel scared."

I found the words to continue. "I'm scared I won't see my kids' faces again."

The surgeon nodded, and I swear I saw her swallow a lump in her throat. Maybe she was a mother, too. Maybe she understood my anguish.. It was simply inconceivable that I might not see my kids' faces again; I just couldn't process this. Mackenzie waited while I wept. The tears slid down my cheeks, and I apologized for crying.

The surgeon walked over to me and put her hand on my shoulder.

"You go right ahead and cry. This is a big fucking deal and you do not need to apologize."

I loved that she dropped the f-bomb; it made me laugh through my tears. While I appreciated her honesty, I struggled with why God or the Universe would do this to me. What had I done to meet this fate? The doctors had ruled out Irish weed, but I still had so many questions, none of which would be answered any time soon.

I checked out of Stanford, dragging my disappointment with me. Nothing had helped. Not a single test or doctor. I felt trapped in the liminal space between hope and despair. Nothing was resolved. So much was left in the balance. And I still had not eaten my taco or drank my beer.

Three days later, my eyesight and life journey would be altered forever.

CHAPTER 4

THE VEIL

ONCE I WAS FREE FROM the hospital, the only things I wanted to do was breathe fresh air, take time to look at the beautiful faces of my three children and husband, and be in their presence as much as I could without being too weird. Strange things were brewing.

My family greeted me at the front door with big hugs and flowers in hand. My mom and sister were there, too. It felt surreal walking into the house. I had the sensation I had been gone for years, when it was really only ten days. But everything had changed. We all knew it, though nobody dared to state the obvious. I was so happy to be with everyone yet I had this feeling of dread and despair. I was home but not home. I was with my family, but I could barely see them. While I could still see in 3D with a small portion of my right eye, at this point my left eye was completely dark. No light was getting in there. Nothing felt familiar. Everything felt familiar. I was stuck in the in-between.

I desperately needed to take a shower, because I felt like I looked like I had just spent a year living on the streets, a mess of greasy hair and dark circles under my eyes. My arms were bruised and covered in what looked like track marks due to all of my IVs and blood draws. I was not a pretty sight. I still had my awesome party favor and tube hanging out of my belly. I would have to cover it with a big piece of plastic so no water would get in.

I stood in the shower and just sobbed for many reasons. While I was so happy and relieved to be home and in my own shower, I was also angry and sad that my future was forever changed. I was desperate to get my eyesight back. I was so deeply sad. Nobody wanted to say anything and I was drowning in my reality, knowing everything had changed.

After what would be one of the last showers I took where I could still see the details of our bathroom, I managed to put on some clothes and find my way back to my family. I took time to sit and hold each one of my kids' faces in my hands and just stare at them. I am sure they thought I was a freak, but I didn't care. I had to take every line of their faces into my memory. I was so scared that when I woke up the next morning all would be dark and lost.

With hesitation I opened my eyes the following morning and was so grateful to still have the small portion of my eyesight intact. I walked into my office and looked at the painting I had been working on when shit went south. I got a gut punch again by life telling me, "You cannot fix this and you have to trust what is coming." My ego responded, "This is fucked up and I don't want to be in this situation!"

That afternoon I went with my husband to watch our boys play a pickup game of lacrosse, which is one of my favorite things to do. My super-fan alter ego comes out when I am watching my kids play sports; my friends named that side of me Jimmy Jams because I talk in my own language and will periodically sing dugout cheers from my softball days or pop off with a voice that is not mine. I suppose it's a fan's way of showing joy. I was thrilled to be out of the hospital and at the game, but I was getting more and more quiet by the end of the game when I began to notice the vision in my *right eye* was changing once again. It was making everything brighter, to the point that it felt like I was not able to keep my right eye open, like when you squint your eyes looking at the sun's glare off the ocean. *What the hell was happening to me?*

It was one thing to see The Spot in my left eye. I really truly wasn't ready to lose the sight in my right eye. But things started to deteriorate quickly. By June 25, my vision had morphed into a strange static. The left eye was still completely dark, but the right eye now had a dense light static over it I had to look through to see. I had no idea what was happening, and I was terrified.

It felt a little like my body and spirit were standing at a fork in the roadmap of my life. Literally one eye contained darkness. The other eye contained light. I did not want to see the black spot. But I was terrified of what the static would do to me—how I'd recover from this "interruption" in my sight. Because let's face it, I was not in a place to accept any of this as permanent. It happened so fast. I prayed one day it would also vanish just as quickly, like an inexplicable rash or a bad dream. I found myself perplexed, literally navigating the details of my everyday life, faced with a choice, it seemed. What was that choice? What was being asked of me? I tried to find the metaphor and squeeze out its meaning. Was I being given a choice to go down the path of darkness in my left eye and continue feeling sorry for myself and give up hope? Or was I to go down the path of the right eye with its bright light and what I would ultimately call "the veil," and not surrender to this strange, surreal event in my life?

I tried to explain it to my family. It wasn't exactly easy. They stared at me, incredulous, while I told them my right eye was shrouded in static and felt as though I was looking at an old-fashioned television screen, the kind of boob tube TV that required antennas to get a clear channel. The problem was I had no "bunny ears" to fix the picture of what I was seeing.

"What do you mean?" they asked me, as if my words had been spoken in Latin.

I tried again to articulate what exactly I was seeing and what I could not see, and my reality began to splinter. Here was the awful truth. I told them I could not see details of anything, even if I held it right up to my eye.

"Can you see our faces, Mom?"

I stood there for a moment holding my breath.

"No," I said. "I know you're there. I can see your shape. But I can't see any details."

Nobody spoke.

We all had the same questions. How could this be happening? What exactly *was* happening? I was their mom. I was a wife. I was a realtor. I had a job. I had duties. I had actions to take, things to do, *every single day*, that were beginning to look like herculean tasks without my vision. I was beside myself with frustration and disbelief.

My family hardly understood, let alone others outside our home. Trying to explain this was the hardest and most frustrating part of seeing people who might not be aware of my condition. I attempted to tell them what was going on with my gut and vision, but it became exhausting. Eventually, I didn't want to leave the house in order to avoid running into friends and telling them my sad story. Debbie Downer was in the house. This was not like me. I was always perky and fun. I could fix and control my environment, but not now.

A few days later, around June 28, I received a call from an ocular inflammation specialist, another doctor I was working with at Stanford. He and my neuro-ophthalmologist suggested a new therapy for my diagnosis: idiopathic optic neuropathy. The word *idiopathic* hit me hard and I had to ask my doctor what it meant. She explained to me that simply put, the cause of my spontaneously onset condition was *unknown*. The other two words simply translated into dysfunction in the peripheral nerves of my eyes. The condition was a vascular one. And vascular conditions were often compromised by inflammation. My gut had been inflamed with diverticulitis. While nobody was connecting the dots just yet, the trail of breadcrumbs was being laid in the midst of a pandemic where mass hysteria was suddenly normal.

But nothing was normal. Working from home and watching my son attend a virtual high school graduation was not normal. While we had the precious gift of time to spend together in ways our modern life made nearly impossible in the past, nothing about our existence in that two-year span was normal. We were surviving a collective trauma, terrified of dying, and knee-jerk reacting to new information on a daily basis. Some of us had the fortune of responding with a more measured approach. Others suffering from pre-existing health conditions had a very different experience. Every day felt like life or death, so it was an easy yes to get the new COVID-19 mRNA vaccine.

It had become the holy grail for so many of us and a game changer for those aged sixty-five and older, who were at most risk. It felt like once the vaccine was available, the world took a collective deep breath it had been holding all year. We were finally going to beat this thing and move on. When it was available for those fifty years and older, I was one of the first people to sign up. I wanted to get vaccinated so I could feel safe against any chance of getting the virus. Plus it would allow me to travel easier without restriction. It seemed like if you had the vaccine, you held a passport to freedom.

What nobody wanted to discuss, however, was whether or not the COVID-19 vaccine might have played any role in further compromising my system. I was so hopeful when the vaccine was available and did not once consider my body might have an adverse reaction. It's not like anyone had a roadmap, and at that time, the data had not yet surfaced for anyone like me to make a more informed decision. Had I known my already inflamed situation might get worse, I would have reconsidered the haste at which I rushed to get this particular vaccine. All I wanted to do was keep myself and others safe. I refused to let COVID-19 cause any more distress to my clients and my business, if I had any say in the matter. Like everyone else, I wanted to move forward with my life and get back to "normal." Fear, not facts, drove me to say yes, without fully understanding the repercussions of my choice. I don't know if anyone else is able to share these thoughts, which were extremely taboo during the pandemic.

I got the vaccine on the one-year anniversary of the infamous shut down, March 13, 2021. It was momentous when the needle went into my arm and the life-saving chemicals entered my body. Though I didn't have any side effects at the time of injection, my body was already in a state of systemic inflammation. One year prior, in May of 2020, I'd had my uterus removed due to chronic fibroids and polyps. Undergoing this surgery during a worldwide pandemic was not the most ideal time. Our family was in flux. My kids were trying to readjust to their new lives in their respective schools with all the daily changes due to COVID-19. My husband was working, and I was trying to figure out how the hell I was going to continue working as a real estate agent when we weren't allowed to go into homes because of the health restrictions facing the industry.

How could I show any clients a home when they weren't allowed to enter it? The stress was mounting for me and everyone else. While my body was adjusting to its wombless self, I leapt at the chance to receive a second dose of the vaccine.

All I could think of while I shoved my sleeve up my arm was that whatever was inside that needle would put all the pieces of my world back together. I wanted to get on with my life and restore my sense of normal like everyone else on the planet. I didn't think twice about my haste because it was what everyone was recommending. I've never used heroin or any kind of intravenous drugs but I couldn't help but wonder if the hope I had when the needle plunged into my left arm was the same felt by a junkie. I wanted instant relief—and safety. I wanted to end my fear and restore my familiarity.

There was no time nor reason to question a few possible outcomes because I had no idea that an unidentified autoimmune disease was already lurking inside me. I did not know to ask if this vaccine might conflict with my autoimmune disease. I did not dare to wonder if this batch contained more proteins than others and would react in a way that would possibly change my life. Nobody questioned it.

When I would ask my doctors if my condition was related to side effects of the vaccine, their answer was always an emphatic no. I wonder if that answer was a result of the social climate and controversy surrounding the vaccine. It felt to me like the shot had provided such hope, no one wanted to confirm any damaging side effects of this life-saving concoction.

All I knew is I had a condition, the actual cause of which nobody understood, hence the word *idiopathic* optic neuropathy. My team of doctors at Stanford recommended immediate treatment with a hyperbaric chamber, which allegedly proved to be a promising treatment for people in my condition. I had heard the term but had no idea what a hyperbaric chamber might offer me. They explained it as a therapy that involves breathing pure oxygen inside a pressurized environment. Hyperbaric chambers were typically used for scuba divers to prevent decompression sickness—a way to treat the deadly bends after surfacing too quickly with nitrate in their blood cells. It was also used for treating wounds caused by radiation, serious infections, air bubbles in blood vessels, and even diabetes—when sugars aren't metabolized and end up like toxic clusters in extremities, which can suffocate oxygen and lead to amputation. I wasn't sure a hyperbaric chamber would restore my eyesight, but they told me it could help fight bacteria and promote healing of optic neuropathy, so I said, "Yes, let's go."

Thankfully, I had already had my party-favor drain removed from my colon, which allowed me to express this emphatic yes. I knew I still had to have surgery, but at least I didn't have this drainage tube coming out of my gut.

Our local hospital fortunately had two hyperbaric chambers, and I was able to get my first treatment the following week. The doctors wanted me to lay in the chamber five days per week, two hours each day. I thought to myself, *I can totally do this! It will give me time to reflect on what has happened and might even be fun.* Yes, I believed this.

Around the first week of July, Stew drove me to my inaugural hyperbaric chamber treatment. Upon walking into the room where the chambers were set up, I was instantly claustrophobic looking at the size of the tube and got the lowdown from the attending doctor and nurse—I would have to endure an environment with three times the air pressure of what's normal. I wanted to run out of the room faster than Flo Jo at the Olympics. But my pride and wanting to see if this would work got the better of me. I changed into the hospital gown, feeling vulnerable in just my birthday suit. The nurse proceeded to explain I could not wear any metal on my body because they would be pumping 100 percent oxygen inside the enclosed tube and the metal could cause a spark, which would be the end of me.

I drew in a deep breath and got on to the hard table that slides into the chamber. It was out of a sci-fi movie and I couldn't believe I was actually proceeding with this. The attendants placed a blanket over me. Before they slid me in and locked the door, they checked the pressure in my ears to make sure I didn't have any blockages, because when they pressurized the chamber, it feels like you're diving deep into the ocean. Your ears slowly equalize and pop for the first ten minutes of the descent. There I was inside this tiny compression chamber, alone with my thoughts, trying not to panic. I'd taken Ativan, my *don't-freak-the-hell-out* pill, an anti-anxiety medication, only ten minutes earlier but it hadn't kicked in yet to help calm me down. I was starting to panic.

As I was laying there in the glass tube of possible death, the nurse spoke to me via speaker asking if I wanted to watch anything on the TV located above my head. WTF? I laughed out loud because that just wasn't an option. Did they not know I was there *because* I was losing my vision? The nurse must have forgotten why I was torturing myself by laying in this glass tube that could explode at any moment. I chose not to tell the nurse and opted to listen to a meditation series on Netflix.

For the next two hours, I tried to "OM" myself into calmness.

At some point, I heard the nurse's voice on the speaker saying I was almost done and needed to ascend slowly. It would take about ten minutes and my ears would pop again as they equalized. Once the door opened and I was pulled out of the glass tube, I felt like a firefly that had just been freed from the jar that everyone would shake to keep from dimming. As I got off the table and was placed on a chair so my vitals could be taken, I was surprised my vision had changed a bit. The colors in the room were brighter and the contrasts were easier to differentiate. I thought, *Maybe this is going to work.*

The next day I went back to the chamber. This time I took my Ativan forty-five minutes before entering, and it helped a bit more. I couldn't stand to listen to the meditation guy's voice telling me to breathe and visualize beautiful green pastures and flowers for another two hours. What I really needed was to listen to a funny and mind-numbing series on Netflix. Thankfully I found it, and subsequently listened to two episodes of the 2012 show *Happy Endings*. Before I actually knew what this show was about I was nervous it might be about a massage parlor and porn. Thank goodness it wasn't.

By the second week of this therapy, I began to dread each visit to the chamber. The claustrophobia had started to take a toll on me. On top of that, I had begun to experience these weird vivid dreams at night: I would be driving a car and lose control on the road, I found myself in a deep hole with someone looking down on me, and I even started seeing friends of mine who had passed away years before. Even worse, my eyes were not getting better at all. After one particular session, my vision was super wonky. The static was darker and more dense. Was this hyperbaric chamber making my vision worse? The doctors wanted to increase the depth, which meant I would have to wear an oxygen mask while laying in the chamber so my brain wouldn't get "messed up," from what I overheard them say. I felt like a test dummy placed in a tube, seeing how far they could go without my head exploding.

After their persistent persuasion, I agreed to go deeper in the chamber, but as I was placing the mask over my face, I had a moment of pure panic. I wanted to get the hell out. I was beginning to listen to my instincts more than before and was considering the alternatives if I got up and left. I had a long conversation with myself and convinced myself to finish the two-hour session. What if this really did help me? I would kick myself if I gave up. Stew and I were always telling our kids to never give up and never surrender. My stubborn nature kept me in the tube, but I will say that once the door opened and I was breathing fresh hospital air again, I wanted to cry with relief. However, my instincts to get up and leave had been right.

As we drove away from the hospital I noticed my vision was even more jacked. I felt like I was hallucinating and thought I saw sandcastles lining the highway. Later that night, I woke up and swore the face of a bald man with a goatee and a big smile was staring right at me, pressed against my face. When I turned to get him out of what I thought was a dream, his face followed me to the other side. What in God's name and green pastures was going on? Little did I know this would be a new chapter in the saga that my life was now becoming. Turns out, the mystery was a journey that my soul was planning to take all along.

CHAPTER 5

WILDLIFE AND BOOBS

BY MID-JULY, I WAS STILL having vivid dreams and daytime visions, but not as often, and the dude with the goatee disappeared. The sandcastles and other weird Dali-esque landscapes remained. No doctors could explain why I was seeing these images. I was not making them up. I was not taking any kind of drugs that might induce such apparitions. Nobody could offer any remedies. My situation continued to perplex the very best and brightest at Stanford.

The only recourse was to undergo an experimental surgery on my left eye to relieve the darkness. It was called a vitrectomy. I said yes. Why not? I was desperate for my situation to change and I would have done anything, short of jumping off a cliff, to save myself, my sight, and my sanity. I was sedated but conscious during the surgery, aware the team was taking the jelly out of my left eyeball and replacing it with a jelly-like saline. They also checked to make sure I didn't have a bacterial infection, leukemia, or an allergy to anything that might cause eye issues. All the tests came back negative. But there was a silver lining. The blessing of this invasive surgery was that the darkness in my left eye was gone and I could now see light. There was no more defining line between the darkness in my left eye and the light in my right eye. It was only light, with the veil shrouding the clarity of my vision in both eyes. I was ecstatic and relieved. Even though I still didn't have vision in my left eye, I could see light instead of darkness.

Following the whirlwind of eye surgery, another medical journey awaited me. Four months into this rollercoaster in 2021, the calendar marked my colon and fistula repair scheduled for early August. It was a bittersweet moment bidding adieu to my peculiar party trick—I'd no longer be recognized as the maestro of on-demand queefs. The surgery and recovery were successful and my surgeon said we had dodged a bullet.

"You look like new, just missing a few parts," he told me on my follow-up visit at his office. He'd had one concern during my surgery, however. My appendix looked suspicious and he went ahead and removed it, too. Why not, right?

Considering my gut was improving after ten treatments in the hyperbaric chamber, this was good news, even though my eyes were not improving. My vision felt forever altered and there was nothing to do but wait.

I was not good at waiting for myself. Although I was patient with everyone else, when it came time for myself, I wanted things to happen now, not tomorrow or three years from now. Patience wasn't something I wanted to cultivate within me, but the mysterious circumstances were dancing with me, refusing to give me what I wanted, when I wanted it. Waiting was going to be the only constant. I didn't like it. I still don't. But fate doesn't look favorably upon those who have not mastered the waiting game. While I hoped and prayed for my vision to return, the Universe had other plans and another calendar.

By mid-September, I was working on accepting my new life with total dependency on everyone around me. The doctors at Stanford had pulled out all the stops regarding my treatment. The only medication I was still on were a few eye drops—including one used for patients with glaucoma—which wasn't me. They threw everything at me like a manic chef tossing fusilli, penne, and paradelle against the wall, hoping one would stick. What I didn't know at the time was that the glaucoma drops stimulate eyelash growth, which was the only silver lining. I knew women who paid a small fortune to get their lashes individually placed during a painstakingly long process only to come out looking like a drag queen. All I had to do was put a few drops in my eyes and, *voilà*, my eyelashes were long and full.

Needless to say, I heard what the doctors were saying, but I felt in my soul there was more I could do to help myself and get my eyesight back to a point where I could see all that I wanted, plus more. What I didn't know at the time was how much more I would actually see once I headed down another path.

I was driven to advocate for myself more strongly as the Western medicine had helped me with my acute condition, but their answers regarding how to heal me were drying up. I reached out to some friends I knew in the world of Eastern medicine. One of those people was my friend Kat, who mentioned she was seeing a craniosacral therapist for some of her own medical symptoms. She suggested it might be something for me to look at to complement the Western medicine treatment I was receiving. She described it as a kind of acupuncture without the needles; it uses a gentle touch to release tension and treat pain of all sorts. I decided to go for it, and it felt great. I was so relaxed and surprised at how well my body reacted to the treatment. Cindy, the craniosacral therapist, held her hands over my fully clothed and blanketed body and used the energy in her hands to work the myofascial tissue (the connective sheath between the skin, organs, muscles, and bones), which plays a big role in the therapy. She worked her way up to my head, holding it in her hands, when my lower back started to twitch. The twitching spread to my entire body and it felt as though I was having a seizure, but I was fully awake, conscious and talking.

I asked Cindy what the heck was happening. She explained that my adrenaline was working its way through my body and releasing any stuck energy. At one moment, I was convulsing so much I wondered if anyone who might walk into the room just then would throw holy water on me to exorcize the demon. It felt and must have looked like something out of a movie, until I realized later through deeper discussion with Cindy that "the demon" was the 6,000 milligrams of steroids I had been given a few months prior to stop the inflammation in my optic nerves. It made perfect sense. The steroids had wreaked havoc on my entire body. I felt so much relief after this first craniosacral therapy and was in awe at how well my body responded. I felt restored. I felt validated. The therapist had released the toxicity that my body could no longer bear. She had healed me. I honestly believe this was the beginning of my new soul path.

After my visit with the craniosacral therapist, I knew I had to continue this type of treatment. Not only had it helped my body calm down, it was helping my vision, too. Every time I left a session, my vision would be just a bit brighter and colors would be crisper. While it was a micro improvement, I was grateful and hopeful. Soon, I found myself seeing a Reiki master as well, who continued to bring my body's energy systems back into balance.

While I was seeing both of these amazing healers, I noticed my eyesight started to look a little different. The static was still there in my visual field, but it seemed to morph into more than just static. Imagine looking at an Etch-o-Sketch that is filled with liquid similar to a lava lamp but with stardust and black fibers floating around in it. The fibers started to create images that were both beautiful but also a little disconcerting. No matter if my eyes were open or closed, I was still seeing these images. And then something completely bizarre happened, which might thrill any heterosexual teenage boy. The fibers and stardust were creating images of women's breasts. All shapes and sizes. And they were literally right up in my face. I had no idea why the hell I was suddenly being shown boobs. Everywhere. All the time.

I mentioned this situation to a female friend and how it was a little weird. Her response was, "Is it, though?" I guess not. We agreed it was better than showing me hairy testicles.

Then came a prophetic turn of events in September. I was starting my journey down the energy healing and Eastern medicine path when a close friend of mine, Bonnie, contacted me to join her and a few other women for a small gathering to discuss life and energy medicine healing.

One of the women in attendance was author Holly Payne, who shared insights into her novel, then titled *Damascena: The Tale of Roses and Rumi* but now re-titled *Rose Girl*. Although I had not read the book, I felt so fortunate to gather with a like-minded group of women who had all undergone a healing journey of sorts and worked in some way as healers, therapists, artists, writers, and executives. It sounded like the perfect event, and I was beyond excited to be included with these women.

I held onto Stew's arm as he walked me into the large barn where we were meeting. It was a bit dark, so my vision was obscured more than normal. I was led to a chair where I sat and felt safe and immediately sensed I had found my people. While we were going around the circle introducing ourselves, I knew I could tell them about the strange images I was seeing in my visual field—not only about the boobs of all shapes and sizes, but about something new that had started to show up: eyes. It was completely bizarre. I told these women I was beginning to wonder if God was playing a sick joke on me. I was losing my central vision only to gain another sight from what people call the third eye, in the center of the forehead, the place I would come to learn was also the Sixth Chakra and is the portal for all humans to see what is considered by many to be "invisible." Call it the spirit world. Call it a hallucination. But I was taking no medicine that would have caused these visions. If only I could have just seen human eyes. That would have been a more familiar place to start "seeing" from my third eye, right? But the eyes I was seeing were not human. No. They were the eyes of animals, specifically lions, tigers, owls, and eagles. I didn't see their bodies, just the eyes of these beautiful creatures, who would passively look at me and then disappear. It sounds nuts. I know. But it was as real as these words that are appearing on the page as I write (or dictate) them. The eyes were not scary or menacing. They made me feel like they were trying to tell me something, protect me, and reassure me everything was going to be okay.

Even though I was seeing these eyes literally 24/7, I had not told anyone else. Nobody in my family was aware of how frequently the eyes showed up. They are there now as I write. I can always see something beyond what once was. And this, at the start, was both terrifying and slightly compelling, though I sensed most people would not have been able to understand this situation or even help me feel at ease with it.

After explaining this to the women, however, I felt a sense of relief and excitement for the first time. They did not feel it was odd. Or strange. Almost everyone gathered in that room believed something larger was happening to me—that I was being invited to see something most of us never do. They likened it to a blessing. I strangely felt a sense of validation as well. I wasn't alone. They were honoring me.

Later, the host, Tara, explained the power and sacredness of rose oil—it emits a high energetic vibration, which is conducive to healing. We were all given a few drops of rose oil to rub between our fingers and then asked, as a display of friendship and love, to place the oil on the woman to our left, gently touching her heart chakra, third eye chakra, and crown chakra.

The entire room smelled like roses. I had the oil on my hands and was wondering how in the hell I was going to place the oil on this gal next to me without poking her in the face. The room was dark and the wildlife and boobs were out in full force. Before I even had a chance to strategize how I was going to anoint the gal to my left, the gal to my right was getting ready to anoint me with rose oil. Instead of placing the oil on my chakra, this beautiful soul knelt in front of me and placed her palms gently over my eyes. A warm and loving feeling came over me at that moment, and while I had no words for it that night, I soon realized it was a spiritual moment. It was as if God placed his hands over my eyes, assuring me everything would be okay. This was similar to the message I was getting from the animal eyes in my visual field. They were all telling me the same thing: this was the beginning of my healing.

I burst into tears when the woman lifted her hands from my face. I was beside myself with gratitude and love. I get chills now writing about it. Spirits, angels, and guides were with me that day. It was amazing. I suddenly understood that what I was seeing in my visual feed was not just wildlife and boobs. It was so much more. It felt like I was looking through a veil and maybe into other dimensions. Because what came next confirmed this—and startled me. While I had lost my central vision in both eyes, I had gained another vision entirely through a third eye.

CHAPTER 6

FOO FIGHTERS READING A BOOK IN SCOTLAND

WHEN YOU LOSE ONE VISION and are given another, there is no choice but to surrender to the unseen forces guiding you to what's next. My life was taking on formidable change well into mid-life. Living near the energetically powerful Ventana Wilderness along the Pacific Ocean, it is no coincidence I was led to meet a reputable shaman in Big Sur who had apparently trained with Peruvians that carry ancient Incan wisdom. He lived at the top of a hill surrounded by beautiful redwood trees and invited me to meet him in his "forest office."

I wasn't sure what to expect because I had never even heard about shamans until this crazy chain of events. However, now that Pandora's Box was wide open, I was all in with meeting and working with healers who could help me in any way, shape, or form. I *was* discerning. This particular shaman was recommended by a trusted, good friend. She would never send me to a quack or creeper. Apparently, this shaman had healed himself from stage four cancer in five organs. Prior to his life as a healer, he was the lead guitarist in a popular '90s rock band. I loved music and figured we could at least connect on this shared passion before he cast any spells.

Upon arriving at the shaman's home, I had no weird gut feeling and felt totally at ease. My husband turned off Highway One and headed east, deep into the bowels of the Ventana Wilderness where the shaman lived with his wife. While I could not make out any details, I knew we were driving deep inside a canyon of old-growth redwood trees. I rolled the windows down and smelled the damp but intensely clean air. It was dark for a while until my husband drove up a hill and I could feel the sunshine on my face through the windshield. Apparently we passed a fire station very close to the shaman's house, which explains why Stew felt perfectly at ease dropping me off. "If anything goes wrong, you're in good hands," he said, noting that his former colleagues were working next door.

I could feel the sunshine all around us but knew we had passed through a thickly wooded area prior, then descended along a narrow and twisting dirt driveway, the tires crushing gravel as we rolled onto the property.

It felt very still and serene when I got out of the car. Although I wasn't sure where we were exactly, I knew we were surrounded by nature. My husband and the shaman shared greetings, then Stew left us alone and drove off the property. It felt like a special place, and I trusted the shaman did his best work here. He was funny and kind, and shared a little bit about his story of how he came to be a shaman. I was grateful to hear how his journey unfolded. As a former rock star, he'd had his highs and lows, but after being given five months to live by his doctors after a stage IV cancer diagnosis, he experienced a calling to help heal other people—as he himself received a miraculous healing from the spirit world. He fully recovered. The doctors had no explanation and still don't. In exchange for his life, he agreed to serve others by facilitating healing ceremonies between them and the sacred land in Big Sur. I was blown away by his story, as I had known many people whose fates ended with a stage IV diagnosis. I was hoping for a miracle myself and literally had my sights set on the shaman restoring my eyesight—as if he was a wizard out of *Harry Potter*. Stew and I did not discuss what the shaman could do for me that day, and I was grateful my husband trusted the situation enough to leave us alone.

The shaman had a loving air about him. He was experienced and professional. I was in awe of him and completely surrendered to his facilitating a healing for me. As we got to work, I shared more about my situation with the eyes and breasts in my visual field and my body's involuntary twitching. He said a beautiful prayer to the four winds, had me visualize what I thought the eyes meant, and then later had me lie on a fallen redwood tree converted into a table with a mat to make me more comfortable.

But comfort was the last thing on my mind. My thoughts were racing. Even though it was the fall of 2021, COVID-19 was still looming and people were still wearing masks. I was vaccinated and felt comfortable not wearing my mask as was the shaman. However, while I lay on the fallen redwood tree table, he said a prayer for me, then blew a liquid, perhaps holy water, over my torso but a few droplets hit my lips.

The first thought that came to my mind was, *Holy shit, COVID!* I kept my mouth shut and played along like nothing was wrong. Of course, after I got off the table I discreetly wiped my mouth. But beyond the droplets hitting my lips, the experience of being surrounded by the majestic redwoods and the spirits of those who had walked that particular land before me was, to say the least, magical. As much as I had secretly hoped that one experience with a shaman would restore my eyesight, the work quelled the twitching in my body instead. My nervous system was shot and the shaman was helping me ground. I was so relieved not to be jerking this way and that. For the first time in months, my body was able to lie still, even on a redwood tree, and my breathing had become coherent. I appreciated the sanctuary and the shaman's bedside manner and was grateful I had come to see him.

He told me that I was becoming a "beautiful butterfly," but I was going to have to sit in the goo for a while to transform. Needless to say, I wasn't super thrilled about the thought of waiting. As I mentioned earlier, I have always been a girl who thrives on instant gratification, and obviously, that was not going to be the case in my current situation. My need for my vision to be restored that day had vanished. My magical thinking went poof.

As I left the shaman that afternoon, I had so many emotions flowing through me. It was such a magical experience and gave me a deeper appreciation for the eyes—if indeed they were trying to tell me something. If the shaman was right, and I was being wrapped inside the silk of a cocoon in order to go through some kind of transformation, I was curious to learn more about the point of all these eyes that continued to visit me. What the shaman was delicately trying to explain was that I would have to dig deep within my soul to unblock myself for my healing journey to begin so I could see my life—and the path ahead—more clearly... if not literally, then metaphorically.

As I moved through the months of July to early September, it was almost as if I was in a holding pattern regarding medical treatment. I was continuing to see the doctors at Stanford on a monthly basis. I was still being tested every month for improvements to the inflammation in my optic nerve. I was also continuing with medications and eye drops, while at the same time exploring more of this energy work and Eastern medicine. The shaman was a one-off, as I felt he had done all that was needed to help me, but I continued with the craniosacral therapy twice per month. I was also beginning to be introduced to others within this energetic healing modality who began showing up to support and help me heal.

At the same time my vision was changing. I didn't gain any clarity, but more eyes were appearing in my visual field—not only the eyes of animals but now the eyes of humans. Initially they were colored and brilliant, like the bright green eyes of the girl from Afghanistan who graced the cover of *National Geographic*. Over time, they lost their color and looked like photographs or sketches in black and white of varying quality. It was almost as if some beings were drawing them for me, and some had more talent to render the details better than others. Some of the eyes were very close up and enlarged, and other eyes looked very far away and would vanish like ether. This would go on and on. Day after day. 24/7. I didn't know where they were coming from. The eyes would just show up uninvited, linger, then leave.

At first, I did not recognize any of them until one day, a pair of eyes showed up that had a distinct familiarity. They were kind, paternal even, and looked very much like my husband Stew's eyes. I was sitting on the couch listening to music and drinking my coffee when these eyes first appeared to me. I froze at first, not afraid, but realizing instantly these were the eyes of Stew's deceased father. It was odd yet beautiful because the way he looked at me was as if he just wanted to tell me he was there with me and that I was not alone.

At first, seeing the eyes was my biggest secret, but when the eyes eventually became human, I told my sister, Sara. I didn't want to freak out my husband so I didn't tell him for a while. Part of me was wondering if these eyes were a figment of my imagination or the effect of some medication. But I was not taking anything and I was not using drugs—recreationally or otherwise—especially after believing The Spot had taken my vision after smoking Irish weed.

After a few weeks of seeing these eyes, I knew deep in my gut I was seeing eyes from the spirit world, both human and animal. I felt like we had a curious connection, like I was a voyeur in another dimension. They were as vivid and detailed as any "scene" I could describe watching a movie; the only problem was that only I could see them. My sister was one of the few people I felt comfortable sharing all the details with beyond the energy healers who were supporting me. They all reminded me that the eyes are the window to the soul. However, it took me almost a week to find the courage to share with Stew about my spiritual sighting from his dad. Even though I couldn't clearly see Stew's facial expression, his verbal response was nonchalant and I'm sure he likely rolled his eyes. After that, we didn't discuss the eyes other than in passing. Stew is a practical man and found it hard to wrap his mind around what was going on. I understood but eventually came to learn how to live with these visits from familiar and unfamiliar spirits, which I had no idea would continue for the next few years.

What I didn't know then is that I was being wound up in a cocoon that would transform me forever. These spirit visits would happen daily and as much as I hoped they would end, I realized there is no time and space. My sense was that the spirits, souls, or angels, or whatever they were, were visiting me for reasons I could not yet understand, let alone explain.

***

After leaving the shaman's table in the redwood forest, I was both hopeful and dismayed. I knew deep down that my original vision was not returning anytime soon. I was on a journey of deep transformation without knowing when it would end. I desperately wanted to speed up the process, but that was not going to happen. I had to find a way to deal with the state of things and be present instead of wishing for the future. If the shaman was right, and I was indeed a "beautiful butterfly," I was going to have to get comfortable with the eyes. I was being forced into an understanding of the infinite—and with it—infinite possibility.

I had to find some aids to help me deal with the chrysalis, like I did when I spent two hours in the tube. I had to find the tools to cope with this distress—and while I did not always find them in prayer at first, I found them in audiobooks and music.

Prior to my condition, I wasn't a big reader, but very soon audiobooks would become my saving grace. I had always been a movie buff and preferred them over reading, but watching movies had become depressing. I struggled to see the screen clearly, and if I hadn't already seen the movie, I would ask a ton of questions, which made it hard for my family to enjoy watching anything with me. I was hurt at first but eventually turned to audiobooks and listened to music to give me variety. I enjoyed sitting outside on our patio with my huge sound-canceling headphones and escaping my life with these stories and songs. One of my favorite audiobook reads was the *Outlander* series by Diana Gabaldon. It helped me escape to the Scottish highlands, as I admired the determination and bad-assery of the Scottish people in the way they fought for themselves. Luckily, I had watched the series with full vision before, which helped me visualize some enjoyable scenes in these books

Another escape for me was listening to music. I had always turned to music to uplift me and could remember the lyrics to most of my favorite songs. When my vision began to fail, I found that music would calm my nervous system, keeping the twitching in my body at bay. There was truth to what I had always sensed about music—certain notes and tones can alter your entire mood. It was a powerful medium and healing modality, and I found myself listening more often than I had prior to my condition. Music by Foo Fighters, Imagine Dragons, Sia, Andy Grammer, U2, and others moved me to tears, which helped release my valve of frustration little by little. It also made me smile and get up to dance, though I hoped I wasn't going to bump into a wall, the drum set in our living room, a table, the dog, or fall into the pool. It felt good and was much-needed medicine for my soul.

While the stories entertained me, the music took me to places I had never explored with my former vision. I've always loved live concerts—I lived for these kinds of events that always fed my extroversion—but I had not experienced music in the way I would after losing my central vision. There was a kind of magic in the music now, and I found myself retreating to our patio rocker, where I would lay for hours, listening to the songs. It truly felt like every song that was playing in my ears via my headphones was the Divine and my angels speaking to me through the words in each of the songs. The lyrics to Foo Fighters' "Times Like These" reminded me that even though we might be going through some shitty times in our lives, we can't give up on ourselves. I listened to that song repeatedly to reassure myself I'd be okay and to keep moving forward. It was songs and music like this that pierced my heart and reminded me to take a breath to ground myself and let go of the pity party that pinned me down in sour moods.

Music uplifted me and it would unwittingly guide me to God. One day, I felt a presence around me as I listened to the song "Angels" by Sia. I was in the bathroom, trying to see myself in the mirror, and started to feel frustrated when all I could see was the static through the veil. I wanted to scream. I was so over this experience and so desperate to see my face and my children's faces, but nothing was changing.

I stepped into the shower and listened to the music while the water washed over me. Sometimes, I would take very long showers because listening to the water allowed me to feel like I was in another world before I had to step out and live again in the world that wasn't quite working for me. I secretly wished I could rub my eyes with the towel while drying off so that, one day, I would open them to see again.

Just as I was having this thought, the song "Angels" started to play on my phone. I was playing the Sia station on Pandora and the song randomly came on and I started to sob in the shower. The lyrics told me to hold on, stay strong, to take an angel by the wings and ask her for a chance to stay, ask her for anything. It reminded me I can do anything and to have faith in what I knew was there but might not be able to see with my eyes. In my case, I was already seeing what most people can't. And now I was reckoning with the "other vision" while the music was awakening me to higher truths.

Over the days and weeks and months that followed, I would lay on our patio rocker and would feel the presence of God and my angels talking to me through the music I was listening to. I knew this might sound nuts, but I also knew there was some truth to it. I had come a long way in determining my relationship with the Divine, and I trusted it.

There was no active progress being made regarding my vision, so I was faced with finding ways to pass the days existing in my new reality. My natural inclination was to fixate on the healing I so desperately wanted, constantly looking toward some amorphous day in the future when I found the answer, when I found what was going to heal and fix me. But this anxiety really was a teacher, reminding me that in this constantly distracted state, I was refusing myself the gift of existing in the present moment. Of loving my life, where I am, right now. This was a new type of time for me. What I found through music and audiobooks was that I was truly the only one who could help myself. Listening to these songs and stories showed me a way to simply be in the present moment. This new form of grounding became my sacred space and a way to truly exist in the in-between moments I had intended to embrace.

CHAPTER 7

WHO'S YOUR DADDY?

AS I WAS INTENTIONALLY living in the in-between, there was ample time for self-reflection and remembrance of how my life story began. Having time to dive into my psyche revealed a common thread—revelations that led me to bring my authentic self into question—between some major events in my life that I had buried deep, which I would later learn can result in acute health trauma.

It is no surprise that the journey of my vision was inextricably linked to my relationship with where I came from. As it turned out, my mom hooked up with a man who would upend everything I ever believed about my identity. I am a blonde-haired, blue-eyed woman who was told she was half Mexican. I relished this heritage, and I believed it was true until I turned thirteen.

My mom was juggling a whole lot raising me and my younger sister as a single parent. She truly wanted the best for us and was doing everything she could at such a young age to take care of her two children. I loved my mom and her quirkiness but was taken aback when she dropped a truth bomb on me one day in the midst of my hormonal upheaval—after getting fitted for my first training bras and navigating the shame of my first cycle of menstruation, while I was being taught to be discreet, to downplay my femininity, to hide my body, and to make sure I was holy, clean, and virginal.

"Jamie, I have a deep, dark secret I need to tell you."

She was driving me to my best friend Iliana's house but gripped the steering wheel of our used Cadillac like she was driving along a cliff... except we were pulling up along the sidewalk of Iliana's house, who happened to be Mexican. She was one of my first friends when we moved to California when I was eleven years old, and we soon became best friends, sharing this unique heritage I thought we had in common.

I couldn't understand my mom's agitation. She seemed nervous. I wondered what secret she could possibly tell me. *Did she eat the whole box of Ho Hos herself?* I looked over at her, anticipating her confession. How bad could it be?

"I don't know who your real father is," she said, looking me in the eye.

The words *real father* made me cock my head. Did I hear her correctly?

Because up until then, I'd had a father and his name was Jim.

"What do you mean my real father?"

My mom was never good at keeping secrets, or so I thought, and spilled the beans like a kid who couldn't hold their pee. She had to let it out.

"I don't know who your biological father is."

I must have given her a look of confusion and disbelief. Maybe on some deep level I knew there was more to this confession than she was willing to share with me at the time. She quickly explained that when she was in her early twenties and took a break from dating Jim, her handsome

Hispanic heartthrob, she met a guy who lived in her apartment complex and they shared an instant connection. Of course. This was the late '60s. The time of sex, free love, and rock and roll. My naive and innocent twenty-one-year-old mom was swallowed up in this wave of love and attention from both men, and ended up getting pregnant with me. When she told them, they both responded, "Not it!"

My mom was too far along in the pregnancy to have an abortion, so she decided she would put me up for adoption. She had no support from either man at the time. As a mother of three children myself, I cannot imagine the enormity of this decision and how terrified she must have been while I was growing inside her.

She struggled with it. Her sisters and brothers and my grandparents offered to take care of me so she wouldn't have to give me up for adoption. They wrote her letters, encouraging her to keep me, and she kept those letters, even to this day.

On the day of my birth in December 1969, my mom decided to continue with the adoption process, even though she was still uncertain about it. Clearly God had another plan for us. The nurses were informed I was going to another family, but one thought otherwise and brought me back into the room for my mom to see and hold. This nurse was my first living angel because my mom changed her mind and kept me.

Six months later, Jim reached out and offered to be a part of our lives, even without real confirmation he was the biological father. While he checked in on my mom from time to time, he did not live with us but offered her the kind of emotional support she needed while she raised me and what would be my half-sister from another man. Jim lived in San Diego and my first memory of meeting him in person was when my mom sent me there to visit when I was eight. While it wasn't uncomfortable, it was definitely an adjustment because I also met his son, Michael, who would become my "brother."

Jim remained a part of my life and still does to this day. Growing up, I called him Dad and believed I was also Hispanic. But on that fateful day when I was thirteen, I experienced an identity split. Who was I if I was not half Mexican? My head buzzed with the discrepancy. This was a complete shock to me because up until this moment, my dad was Jim. He was Mexican. I prided myself on being half-Latina. Even though I had blonde hair and blue eyes, I believed I was more Spanish and that was why I had the coloring I did. I had the crazy thought that maybe two sperm fused together when they entered my mom's egg. It was such a weird thought, I know, but I was only thirteen years old and didn't have the capacity to process what my mom had just shared with me. I continued to live my life as half-Latina and was proud of it, too.

However, during the next five years, I wondered every day who my actual father was until my mom mentioned a small detail: oh, he went to the same high school as you.

I ran with it. At eighteen, and being that it was my senior year, I could not help myself and dug up old yearbooks with my friend Carolyn. Our analog search criteria was to find yearbooks for when he might have graduated. And sure enough, we found a photo that would confirm the truth.

"What do you think?" I asked her.

She studied the photo, looking closely at the cute blue-eyed young man beaming a smile.

"Holy shit!" she said. "He looks a lot like you!"

I didn't want to believe it and snapped the yearbook closed, then stuffed the memory deep into my subconscious. Thirty years later, the memory resurfaced and I found myself needing to know who he was in January 2020, when I was fifty years old. Call it a mid-life crisis, but my soul demanded I finally know the cold, hard truth. I took a DNA test through Ancestry, wondering if the man in the yearbook photo would match. When the results arrived in my email, I waited at least a week to open them.

I sat at my laptop, staring at my inbox, feeling my heart pound. I was wrestling with the truth. Part of me did not want to know, while the other part desperately needed to know who I really was. I finally took a breath and clicked on the email to learn the truth: I was not half-Latina after all. I am Scottish and Irish. This revelation was a complete blow to my identity. I always took pride in being a woman of color, although my Black and Mexican friends lovingly laughed at me with my blonde hair and blue eyes. I tried to prove I was more like them when I had a really good tan. But still, the tender taunting and rolled eyes continued. All jokes aside, all my life I'd believed I was something I was not. This was not easy to digest when I was thirteen and even harder to process in mid-life—by then I had coopted that identity for decades. I mourned my lost Mexican heritage.

I sat there reading the DNA results and made the decision to keep this to myself. I didn't want my mom to feel badly, but soon after I had received the confirmation of my Scottish-Irish heritage, she asked me if I'd ever taken one of the DNA tests. To make the situation more surreal and uncomfortable, we were in the car driving to my mom's favorite Mexican restaurant, of course.

"You mean like Ancestry or 23andMe?" I asked her, thinking this was an odd turn in the conversation. We were just ordering our lunch out loud, fantasizing about our favorite items on the menu and a mother-daughter mid-day margarita.

It felt strangely like the day we sat in her used Cadillac driving to Iliana's house. I sensed from the way she was talking that she wanted to tell me the truth or have me tell her what I had already discovered on my own. I couldn't lie.

"Yes," I said but didn't take my eyes off the road.

"Which one?"

"Ancestry."

There was a pause as we continued to approach the Mexican restaurant, the irony not lost on either of us. She took a deep breath, just like she had years ago.

"What did it show?"

"Well, I am not Mexican, and Jim is not my biological dad."

She swallowed the truth and nodded. "I know," she said.

I gripped the steering wheel but turned to her with a look that must have come across like, *What the actual fuck!?*

"You mean you knew this whole time and let me live this lie?"

"Yes, but I figured you knew by now and were okay with it."

I felt the heat of anger roll through my body. No, I wasn't okay with it. I told her I was struggling. It had been a hard reveal, much harder than I thought, and the reason for my staunch hesitation to take the test all along. I told her I could never tell my childhood dad, Jim. Then she cold-cocked me with yet another brutal disclosure.

"Jim knows, too."

"Knows what?" I asked, feeling my chest tighten.

"That you aren't his biological daughter."

"What the hell, mom?! How long has he known?"

"Since you were a baby," she confessed.

This hit me even harder in the gut than I realized. I felt so many emotions at once: anger, deception, sadness then gratitude, love, and a twinge of abandonment. Needless to say, it was not the typical fun mother-daughter lunch we anticipated. I don't remember much of what happened after this huge reveal, only how I felt.

No wonder my anxiety kicked into high gear and my blood pressure slowly crept up. I was gearing up for a showdown with my ego and wasn't prepared to fight. This was going to be a long lunch. I made sure to drink a strong margarita when we arrived at the restaurant, where my mother flirted with the men of color she'd always loved while I realized the only White guy she'd ever dated was my birth father.

***

Later, I would use the technique of screaming into pillows to process and release years of being in survival mode and other emotions I had pushed down for decades. I thought about my Mexican dad, Jim, and how blessed I was to have him in my life. He didn't have to take on the responsibility of helping to raise me. Even though he and my mom never got married, he was there when I needed him and still is to this day. I am forever grateful for his love and support. My mom has always been such a beautiful and free spirit. She took on the role of mother to a baby girl she wasn't sure she could really care for and raised me with so much love in a family that truly cared about me. I am so grateful to them that it brings tears to my eyes. As for the other guy, the White guy, the sperm donor/birth father, Dennis, I was grateful he hooked up with my mom and gave me life. As the Scots say, "Solange," cheers.

This experience in witnessing the flawed humanity of my parents would be a valuable lesson to keep with me as I began to navigate the forgiveness of my own human flaws.

CHAPTER 8

DON'T SAY THE B-WORD!

IN THE PERIOD BETWEEN September and November of 2021, I spent the months struggling to live day to day with my visual impairment. Routines were very different, and my dependency on others was necessary. I hated it. I was doing my best to keep my head up and stay positive, but there were days when I felt paralyzed by my condition. The final visit for the calendar year with the neuro-ophthalmologist and the infectious eye doctor at Stanford Eye Center didn't improve my outlook.

"Your optic nerve is still inflamed a bit, so we are going to keep you on the eye drops and the medication that makes your hair fall out, too. You can stop with the nuclear drugs, though, so that's good news," they reiterated, then added without irony, "Oh, and we still don't know what caused your visual impairment."

I sat there stunned yet not surprised. They were not telling me anything I didn't already know. In fact, they were repeating what all of us knew, which wasn't much. I wasn't sure what I was hoping to hear from them, but the blunt admission that they knew nothing more about the cause of my condition left me in a daze, until my neuro-ophthalmologist mentioned getting on the list for a guide dog.

I did not realize the offront of those two words. *Guide. Dog.* It's not that I didn't like dogs. I loved dogs. We already had two dogs—I didn't need another one. Maybe God really did have a sense of humor, but there was no way we could handle a third dog.

"A guide dog?" I asked, wondering if this doctor was joking.

"Yes. You should put your name on the list now. It can take a while."

I drew in a sharp breath. "What list? Whose list?"

She cleared her throat. "The organization, Guide Dogs for the Blind."

She had said the word I refused to say.

Blind. I was not blind. I was barely visually impaired.

All this was temporary, didn't she know? I refused to see myself as blind. I could see light. It was not all darkness. I would not call this place or put my name on their list.

"The only dog I'm getting will be the one I take on runs with me," I said.

I got up and walked out of the office. The word *blind* made me tense, and I felt a wave of anger. I was not blind. I was visually impaired. And while I appreciated her suggestion, as though she were telling me I might start thinking about a prosthetic limb as if I'd lost one, I wasn't ready to put my name on the list.

My eyes still worked. I wanted to tell her about the veil. I wanted to tell her about the eyes I *was* seeing. While I might not be able to see in vivid detail everything that was in front of me, and, let's face it, could no longer drive or walk on my own or do much of anything on my own without assistance, I refused to take a service dog from somebody who might need it more. The only list I wanted to show up on was the one that included the miraculous return of my central vision. How do you politely tell a medical expert you disagree with her because you had lost one kind of vision but had gained another—and a service dog wouldn't help or change that situation one iota?

The more I thought about some of the other organizations she'd told me about to help someone in my condition, like the Blind and Visually Impaired Center, on my way home from the appointment that day, I scoffed, wondering what they could really do for me. I had three children. I knew for sure I did not want another responsibility with a dog.

I continued to navigate the vagaries of my medical appointments with others on my team. While most visits with the neuro-ophthalmologist lasted an hour, the infectious eye doctor meetings lasted for hours. Granted, he was world-renowned and I was fortunate to have him on my case, but he would hold me there for four to six hours per visit, putting me through a barrage of tests that included looking into a box with a lens while trying to focus on a bright spot I could not see, taking pictures of my optic nerve, retina, and macula while I was told not to blink. I felt like a robot.

My favorite test was one where they placed probes under my eyes and then stuck a cone on my forehead with Silly Putty. They connected the probes, which were actually small sticky strips of paper that looked like something that would go into a computer chip. Once everything was on, the technician stuck a hand-held magnifying glass in my hand and told me to put it up to my eyes, one at a time. I looked like a total misfit unicorn, but I didn't care. The technology was going to help me in some way, shape, or form, God willing.

I was told to look through the magnifying glass as the music played, without blinking once until the song ended. The test was a killjoy to my love of music. Not blinking for an entire song is a lot harder to do than you think. While the music played and my eye was pressed against the magnifying glass, the only thing I could think about was the children's television show from the '70s called *Romper Room*. Miss Nancy would look into the magnifying glass and say, "Romper, stomper, bomper boo. Tell me, tell me, tell me do. Magic Mirror, tell me today, did all my friends have fun at play?" Then she would call out children's names at the end of the show. I would watch each episode, hoping one day she would say my name along with everyone else's. I decided to dedicate one of those eye tests to Miss Nancy and say my name while looking through the glass. Looking back, maybe all I needed during those excruciating hours of being tested was for someone to see me trying to see. There is an inherent loneliness I began to experience as a patient and it made me think of everyone who had to show up for these kinds of tests—or any other—that are central to the investigation into the cause, and possible cure, of this condition.

While I know these tests are part of this particular specialist's procedure, at times I sensed he might be messing with me. He seemed to have a sense of humor. Upon my initial visit, I had to fill out the typical health history form but because I could not fill it out, Stew had to fill it out for me. In the spirit of the cult classic *Harold and Maude*, he was asking me the questions on the form and filling in my answers, until one section got a little tricky. It asked if the patient had ever had certain venereal diseases. These included warts, herpes, and syphilis, and I said no to all of those. When he asked about chlamydia, I paused and my mind whizzed. If I told him the truth, he might freak out. But if I withheld the truth, I might be blatantly thwarting the investigation if, indeed, a VD might have something to do with impacting someone's eyesight.

He asked me again. I finally uttered, "Yes."

Stew dropped the pen, which carried its own voice that said, "WTF" until it landed on the floor. My husband didn't bend down to pick it up but I felt him turn to me.

"Really?" he asked, clearly flabbergasted.

"Yes, really," I said and shrugged. I was twenty-one years old when it happened, I explained, and had never had a VD since.

Stew picked up the pen and checked off chlamydia.

Just then, my ocular inflammation specialist walked into the room with his posse of colleagues in pursuit, including an undergrad student, a doctor from Vietnam, and a doctor from South Korea. I didn't need a dog to tell me they were there. Through the veil, I could see their forms, and I knew they had come to observe and learn from my doctor, who was sitting at his computer.

After the VD roll call, Stew was in a chair in the corner and wanted to bolt. The room was small, and I felt like I was in the middle of a mush pot. My doctor looked over my health history without saying a word. The room was silent for what felt like an eternity.

Finally, he spoke, "So, the chlamydia, was it a while ago?"

Stew made a sound that sounded like a stifled laugh, while the three doctors staring me down were leaning in to hear my answer, in case I didn't say it loud enough. *Why the hell did we have to focus on that one box with all the others to discuss?*

I felt my cheeks flush and answered with an honest, "Yes. It was a long time ago! Satisfied?" I could sense he had a slight grin on his face when I answered. He didn't ask me any other questions about my health history form and to this day, I still have no concrete knowledge of a venereal disease affecting eyesight.

I was wiped out after that visit to the Stanford Eye Center. It was a full day, like most visits, and I just wanted to get home and sleep. I needed to rest because my two older kids were coming home for the holidays and I didn't want to be a sloth and not have the energy to be with them. While I was determined not to get a dog, I kept thinking about the Blind and Visually Impaired Center. I made a deal with myself and Stew—I would check it out and see if they could help me.

I eventually contacted our local Blind and Visually Impaired Center and made an appointment with the optometrist who volunteers for the organization. I wanted to get this over with and was able to get in to see her before Christmas, but we met another dead end. While they offered volunteer services to help navigate my new reality, they offered little with regard to helping my eyesight, despite all the technology, giant magnifiers, and other pieces of equipment they have available to their community. I didn't realize at the time how resistant I was to this type of assistance, because that acceptance would imply acceptance of my disability.

I just wanted to go home and be with my thoughts and sadness. The kids were all under our roof once again and I was beyond happy to have all my little chicks home for the holidays. Christmas is typically my favorite holiday, but that year it was particularly hard not only because my kids' faces were shrouded by the veil but also because I couldn't get in my car, drive to the mall, or go online and scour websites for the perfect gifts for them. I had to rely on others to take me shopping, explain to me what was available, and then help me put in my credit card or hit purchase on the computer. Shopping usually brought me great joy, but it had suddenly become depressing.

The other dilemma posed by Christmas was that we have a tradition where we don't place any gifts under the tree until Christmas morning. I would usually hide the gifts somewhere, then on Christmas Eve, I would stay up late and shuttle all of the gifts under the tree. Then I would fill the family stockings on the fireplace mantel. I was so delighted and found joy in playing Santa Claus. But not that year.

I had to let my husband and kids do all the decorating, wrap the gifts, and place them under the tree. I had no control over what was happening, and I didn't like it. But my family is a pretty special and amazing bunch and helped recreate what I did every year so that it would hopefully have the same feelings as if I did it with them, too. One bright spot of that Christmas was the mere fact I realized my family was as tight-knit as ever. My love for them filled my heart so much that the day ended up being one of the best holidays we had ever had, and I will cherish it forever.

Once the older kids went back to their respective colleges, I was happy to see 2021 end. I was hopeful 2022 would bring good news about my eyesight, and I was definitely ready to shift from sad, flat, pissed-off Jamie to the positive, loving, happy, and clear-eyed Jamie. I didn't ever want to hear the B-word. I know that word was used when friends and family talked to each other about my condition. Obviously, I was in denial, and I had a hard time surrendering, but I knew that in order to get better I needed to do just that. It was going to be harder than I thought. Surrendering would demand that I dig deep to change my entire life for the better. Change was the only certainty. For now, however, I was still deep into the bargaining stages of my condition—believing that if I just found the right healer, with the right potion, then I just might regain my sight.

CHAPTER 9

TRUE NORTH

THE NEW YEAR OF 2022 began with equal hope and desperation. I was grasping at straws trying to understand my condition when nobody else seemed to have the answers. I was still working with Stanford, but the appointments were getting fewer and farther between, going from monthly visits to once every three months. It felt like they were distancing themselves from me as it became more apparent they didn't understand the causes of my vision loss or how to fix it. I still had inflammation in my optic nerve, which meant I was still not healing. Without the comfort of a committed or consistent team to guide me through, I realized I was on my own. I was terrified and frustrated.

In early March 2022, I reached out to my friend Amy Scher, author of *How to Heal Yourself When No One Else Can*. Her book offered helpful techniques to work with your conscious and subconscious as a way to deal with various ailments—especially those that go undiagnosed or, in my case, don't fit into any box despite great efforts to define their cause and their treatment. I took in all her words and was taking them and anything the Universe sent me as a message. When Amy mentioned a doctor in Brooklyn she thought might be helpful in getting answers to my situation with my eyes and gut, I knew I had to see him. New York is only a short 3,000-mile cross-country trek from my home in California, but at this point no distance could deter me from finding the answers to getting my eyesight back.

As luck would have it, I was able to get an appointment and go with a little help from my friend Maria and my daughter, Mackenzie, my travel buddies. We flew into JFK on a Thursday to kick off our four-day Vision Quest. Mackenzie and I arrived at the office together, while Maria was scouting out places to meet later that evening in Brooklyn. Despite our high hopes, my meeting with the doctor was a little lackluster. He was very knowledgeable and found that my pH was off in my gut but had nothing helpful to say regarding my eyesight. It was a bit disappointing but I chalked it up to leaving no stone unturned when it came to having trusted healthcare professionals give me their opinions. At this point, it wasn't about a second opinion but a tenth and twentieth. I was determined to stay open to hearing what others had to say, and if they provided even one clue into the "why" of my ailment or could offer any helpful advice or wisdom, I considered it worth the effort.

The point of the trip was not about the doctor. My daughter reminded me the point was to be "normal." To not let what was happening to my vision impact my ability to fully participate and enjoy my life. I loved to eat, drink, and be merry, so Mackenzie and Maria refused to see me any other way. New York was about the in-between moments, spending time with these two amazing and beautiful women. We laughed our asses off, ate super yummy foods, and felt like we were in an episode of *Sex and the City* when we hung out in Carrie's neighborhood. We even went to a wedding in Long Island and had drinks at Heath Ledger's bar in Brooklyn where we met Coco, a visual effects producer for movies. She was working on a film in Brooklyn for Amazon. She was hilarious and maybe a little drunk and high, but sure made for great conversations.

We ended up meeting Coco the following evening after attending the musical, *Music Man*, starring Hugh Jackman. She wanted to know how we liked it. Although I couldn't see the actors on stage very well, I told her that listening to the music and just being in the theater was enough. She smiled and nodded, "You get it." I loved her. The irony was not lost on any of us because she was a visual effects producer and yet she understood the point was not to just see something but to experience the sum of it.

The last night we were in New York, the girls passed out early, and I was left alone with my thoughts. I was still wide awake, energized by the show and Coco's insight. Maybe I did get it or was getting it, but it felt great to have someone bear witness to my effort. I sat there in bed for a few moments thinking about Hugh Jackman's voice and smiled, wondering how many more shows I might be listening to instead of seeing. Over the months, I had slowly shifted my form of entertainment and had become used to listening to everything I once saw. That said, I knew I'd be up for a few more hours and was considering listening to an audiobook and texted my friend Lauren, who recommended I read a book about a New York Times reporter who had lost his sight. I sent her a text, via voice, of course, and she texted me back, being three hours behind in California. I listened to Siri read her message: *The Beauty of Dusk* by Frank Bruni. I wanted to download the book right then, which I normally would by using Alexa at home, but I had not become savvy enough with my phone to have it download for me. Each day was an endeavor in learning new adaptive technologies to assist me. I was on a massive learning curve. That said, I didn't have a book to listen to, so I felt around on my nightstand for the remote so I could unmute the TV, which was flashing lights as commercials changed before me.

I love comedy and late night shows, so I was happy to land on *The Tonight Show with Jimmy Fallon*. They said the original show had been taped around Thanksgiving, but I didn't care because I hadn't been able to listen to his show at all in the last year; I was totally down to watch a rerun. What happened next still leaves me speechless and gives me goosebumps. While my daughter and Maria snored peacefully, I turned up the volume slightly when I heard Jimmy Fallon introduce his next guest, Frank Bruni. *No way,* I thought. The Universe had my full attention. He was on the show to talk about his book, *The Beauty of Dusk,* which was about his diagnosis with a severe visual impairment. I laughed out loud and was beside myself, with chills all over my body. Clearly, I was meant to read his book. It took getting me to New York to know this.

The next morning, I asked Mackenzie to help me get the book on my Audible app. While we were waiting for our ride to take us to the airport, I started to listen to the book. I barely got through the first eight pages before I burst into tears.

Both Maria and Mackenzie were a little surprised at my emotions.

"OMG, are you okay? What happened, Mom?"

I couldn't stop crying, and when I finally caught my breath, the words flew out of me. "He is saying everything that I was feeling when I learned of what was happening to me when I started to lose my eyesight," I explained. "It's like he had the same feelings I did when seeing the doctors for the first time, when he saw their faces and the grim looks they gave him, how he was trying to convince himself that what was happening was not real."

Mackenzie said she had chills. Maria hugged me. They didn't know what to say. I wiped my tears and drew in a deep breath, wondering how on earth this had come full circle. Frank Bruni was telling my story, too—the only difference was he had not gained another vision with his "third eye." I didn't care. Every word rang true. He had articulated what I had not yet been able to, and it gave me comfort to know someone else was going through this, too. His book made me feel less alone, became a companion, and motivated me to share my story someday, too, so that somebody else might feel seen. And trust me, the irony was not lost on me: being seen by the visually impaired was possible.

When I finally pulled my shit together and we headed to the airport, I came to the conclusion that this trip was really meant for me to know that I wasn't alone in this messed up situation. The spiritual world was giving me companions—and signs.

***

After returning from New York, I had a hunger to understand what was happening and found myself diving into books about energy healing, intuitive healing, and… let's just call it the world of woo-woo. It wasn't just the signs I wanted to understand better; I was still grappling with the daily appearance of the eyes I continued to "see" with my third eye. This was becoming so routine, yet I continued to live through it mostly in silence, not discussing it with anyone beyond a select few. I knew I needed to find more support outside of our home to help me navigate this situation. I was clearly being pulled into another world and it frightened me, but I was determined to overcome my fears and find a way to understand why the hell I was seeing these things yet still unable to see my children's faces in any detail. Or drive. Or have any kind of independence other than finding my way around our house without a stick or a guide dog. I was dependent on everyone but desperately wanted to find my own way forward. It would require letting go of everything I once thought was true about how the world operated, what I once saw in detail versus what I was seeing that nobody else could.

As I reset my compass to my new truth north, I discovered the podcast *The Jen Weigel Show* and found myself loving her interviews with a myriad of mystics, mediums, psychics, and healers, along with others who shared inspirational stories and messages. They spoke of mysteries and surrendering to the unknown. They sounded resolved in their circumstances, which baffled me at first and equally intrigued me. How could people find a way to accept what was? It seemed to be a recurring theme in these podcast episodes, and I soon released my skepticism and settled into my happy place learning about this new world and those who lived in it. I felt like they had messages for me if I listened closely and if I got quiet enough to connect the dots.

Slowly, as I listened to the stories and books, I started to make sense of my childhood history. While I navigated the day-to-day adjustments of living as a visually impaired person — hurtling across the ever-evolving learning curve of using technology and learning how to accept my limitations while simultaneously overcoming them — I realized my past had truly impacted my present. Then I started to get very quiet, considering some truths that were pushing up like dandelions in cracked concrete. Something was growing inside me that wished to be known. I listened to more podcasts and audiobooks. I stayed aware. Hungry to know more. Why? I was being prepared.

The Universe was ready to reveal yet another big secret of my life.

***

Shortly after returning from New York, my mom was driving me to a hair appointment and we were talking about her youth and how she dealt with being a young and single mother. She told me a story about her friend Toni, who would watch me when I was three years old. My mom went on to tell me she would occasionally get a call from Toni saying she couldn't find me in the house.

"Where was I?" I asked.

My mom said nothing.

"We didn't know. That's the point."

I sat in the car while she drove, letting this sink in.

"Hmmm. Isn't that funny and freaky at the same time?"

She said it was, but in my mom's fashion, she didn't seem fazed.

"It turns out that one time you decided that you wanted to take a walk with our dog and left the apartment to do just that."

All of a sudden, I remembered the day. I realize it's hard to remember anything before the age of three but I got chills as the details, though blurry, resurfaced the more my mom shared. I'd taken Coco, our mutt, who was bigger than me as a labrador mix, out the front door of our apartment. I don't remember if I was wearing shoes but realized it was likely I was in bare feet. I padded out the door along the concrete walkway with Coco guiding me to the stairs and proceeded to walk down them and across the parking lot to the sidewalk that led to the ice cream truck. I loved ice cream. I loved my dog. What was there to be afraid of? I sat there in the car while my mom continued, feeling an odd sense of peace about this incident.

She then recounted another time when she took me to the laundromat at six months old and struck up a conversation with a woman who had a young child as well. They hit it off and she felt safe enough to drop me off at her house the next day. My mom confessed she was struggling to find good childcare while she was at work and felt comfortable bringing me to this woman's house knowing almost nothing about her except that she had limited English. Lucky for all of us, she turned out to be a kind and loving person. My mom needed help and it showed up.

When my mom recounted these two incidents, I wasn't alarmed. If I did this today, I would probably be ostracized and maybe even questioned about being a fit parent. My mom was fit, tuned into her deeper sense of knowing, and made a judgment call based on sensing this woman, while a stranger, would never harm me. She was right. And while she reminded me, I felt calm, remembering something I had forgotten for years.

No matter what circumstance we had found ourselves in, we almost always felt safe. I believe something was always there protecting us. Watching over us, perhaps. Though we never talked about it, our lives were blessed by angels—seen and unseen.

***

I continued my investigation into my past. Through podcasts. Audiobooks. Anything I could hear. My ear also deftly tuned into what was *not* said, what was possibly implied between the lines—and the life I had lived prior to the diagnosis and the one I found myself living then. It certainly helped to listen to the thoughts of others whose perspective I would have never considered prior to my diagnosis. With not a single doctor from the hallowed halls of Stanford able to tell me why this had happened, I was left to figure it out, and it sure as hell was clear the answer did not exist inside a medical textbook. I was starting to open myself up to the possibility that something was governing this situation—condition—disability—for my own growth. And lordy, that was hard to swallow. It's not an easy thing to accept. I was only in the early stages of awareness, but the needle in my compass was showing me a new true north.

Here's the deal. I don't believe my visual impairment—and my ability—to see the unseen began when I was fifty-one. Looking back, I had already developed an ability to see the invisible world from a very young age even though I didn't know it then. The day Coco guided me to the ice cream truck, I felt nothing but joy and anticipation. I had no fear of being guided, and I believe Coco was the first embodied angel in my life. There was no mistaking that I had recently met another Coco that night in Brooklyn when I stumbled upon Frank Bruni on *The Tonight Show with Jimmy Fallon*. This is what I mean when I say I had to get quiet to connect the dots. I had to go inside to see for the first time what was real and what was true for me. It turns out I did not need my central vision to feel the presence of my angels. When I left my apartment as a little girl that day to walk the dog alone, I never felt scared. The angels were with me. They still are.

I explained this to my mom and to others who came to help me during this time of growing awareness. A few months prior, I had been introduced to a healer named John Newton through my friend Sarah, who knew I was deep into my despair and loathing. She had trained under him, so I could trust her own development and his skills. He was known for ancestral clearing, which was a fancy word for saying he could help me reach way back in my family history to sort out a few things that might be connected to my new ability to see "eyes." John had a sense of humor, too, and was a former movie and TV actor who pivoted careers so he could focus solely on ancestral clearing. He sounded eclectic and interesting, so I thought I'd give him a shot.

Our first call lasted only twenty-five minutes but he mentioned some of the most significant events of my childhood that had shaped who I had become. I was dumbfounded. *How did he know all this? Had my friend tipped him off?*

No. She hadn't. And it didn't matter how he knew. He was right.

So right that he helped me understand more than any doctor I had met.

***

The first thing we discussed was why my gut was having a hissy fit. Recall the diverticulitis I was dealing with leading up to smoking the joint in a Denver hotel before I first saw The Spot? My belly had been through some stuff. Not just recently, either. John asked me if there was ever a time when I felt alone or afraid. Though my mom's recent confession helped me remember I had angels, I also remembered I had not always felt herculean. It made sense. I had been a very little girl.

"Yes," I said.

He prompted me to explain when, where, and how old I had been.

The memory flooded me. It's almost as if just focusing on my belly, the place where I had pushed so many emotions, opened up Pandora's Box.

And while what I was about to tell him wasn't exactly a happy memory, it surfaced easily, as though my entire body had been waiting for years to expel it. My poor belly was full. It wanted to be released of its duty to hold so much for so long.

I shared with him that the first thing that came to my mind was when I was eight years old. We were living in Kansas where my mom was working at least two jobs to support us, which meant my sister was three years old and in childcare full-time.

I would get dropped off by the bus from school, walk to the daycare place to pick my sister up, and babysit her until my mom came home from work. On this particular day, I waited to pick my sister up because I wanted to have a bowl of sugar cereal (a treat for us). While enjoying my sweet bowl of kid goodness, I heard the phone ring and proceeded to pick it up.

It was my mom. She sounded a little flustered and said I needed to get into the basement because there was a tornado warning and the basement was the safest place for me to be. At first, I wasn't sure I liked hearing my mom say this. I did not want to go down into our dark, dank basement alone. Basements were always a scary place and it was the last place I wanted to be in a storm without anyone in the house.

As she spoke, my first thought was, *I wish the phone wasn't working.* Our phone was often disconnected when I was a kid because Mom fell behind on payments as she navigated the day-to-day needs of taking care of all three of us on her own. Thinking back, I am so glad our phone was working that day. While I sat alone in the basement, I made sure the phone was with me, even though I didn't know who I would call if anything happened. I kept thinking about how scared I was being by myself and if I was going to fly away in the house like Dorothy in *The Wizard of Oz.* I clutched the phone and my knees to my chest, frightened about what might happen to my sister while she was away from me. My trembling eight-year-old self wanted to protect her but didn't know how. I knew she was in the best place at daycare, but I selfishly wanted her there with me so I wouldn't be alone.

I had not thought about this day for years. In fact, I think I stuffed it deep inside my gut so I wouldn't have to think about it. I was terrified. John's question swung open that door. By asking if I had ever been scared, alone, afraid, or felt abandoned, I discovered that the answer was, in fact, yes, I had been terrified for years.

It turns out I had been in a trauma loop ever since this incident, and I held so much of these emotions in my gut—the third chakra, he explained, helping me understand why my gut was so compromised for most of my life. He helped me process and clear the fear. He helped me let go of a lot of shame and anger, which began in that basement with a tornado looming, when I did not know when or if my sister or mom would be home or if they were safe.

After my call with John, I sat there in awe of what had just happened. I was astounded. It all made sense. I felt relief and grief simultaneously for all I had endured and saw the grit and resilience I had developed as a result, including my ability to listen to my spirit. The memories started flooding back and the message I heard was I have guides and angels who are always near me, even though there were many times in my life when I didn't feel them. All this was great, but it opened a proverbial can of spiritual worms.

CHAPTER 10

EVERYTHING IS FINE

I WANTED TO BELIEVE that everything was fine—or that it would be fine someday. Some days I did. Others I didn't. The journey to fine was a fickle line I followed every day. It zigged and zagged and I found that my hearing was growing more acute when I could not see the details of the life around me. Comically, while I could hear my dog fart, the smell was heightened as well. Nature truly abhors a vacuum, I realized, and it was filling in the gaps fast. The entire situation was hard to process so I turned to music, which had always calmed me down, lifted my spirits, and made my heart happy.

I began to play a little game with music, finding the words in songs that spoke to me of my condition. It was perhaps a bit like using songs as a sort of I Ching, a path to divination, anything to give me signs of what was happening and heading my way. One day when Mackenzie approached me about songs she might sing with her band, I chose the Tracy Bonham song from the '80s, "Mother, Mother!"

She asked me why this song and I explained that the chorus, "Everything's fine," resonated because it speaks to how I felt going through the hardest challenge of my life.

Besides, I loved the fierceness and rage Tracy Bonham put into this particular song. Her sarcasm is biting, and it was exactly how I often felt.

This song perfectly mirrored my inner chaos, especially the wonkiness of my eyesight. I chose the term *wonky* deliberately, resisting a label that would make any of this seem real, when in fact, it was all *surreal*. When I saw friends or met people for the first time, I felt the urge to explain myself and tell them why my gaze might look funny or why I might not be looking directly at them. The insecurities continued to escalate, which was so unlike me. I was talkative and outgoing but found myself withdrawing more and more in social situations. It's not because I didn't want to talk to people, it's that I was constantly thinking about how fucked up my eyesight was, especially when I was always having to look over people's shoulders to see their face or full body, relying on the little bit of peripheral vision I still had left. I thought about getting a tattoo that said "Shifty" or "Here's looking at you side-eyed" so that people could understand me better. At least my humor could hide what I was feeling, until that game exhausted me, too. The solution, I found, was to avoid any interaction with people whatsoever.

I found myself in a precarious performance that oscillated between genuine connection with others and the fear of being perceived as inauthentic because I was so preoccupied with what they thought of how I looked. I was in no way ready to admit I was blind, but I could fake seeing them for as long as possible. The song spoke to the tightrope I navigated with each encounter that forced me to face my situation.

After my daughter listened to it the first time, she looked up and asked, "Is everything fine, Mom?" And we both laughed, knowing damn well it wasn't.

I was struggling day after day with my situation. While my family had not had a single conversation to address what had happened and what was happening, aside from my cascading jokes, nobody was in a good headspace. Worse, half were in denial. My husband and oldest son, Hayden, chose to avoid any kind of conversation directly related to my situation. Stew had been a firefighter and was a master at compartmentalizing conflict. Hayden followed suit. Both were avoiders, refusing to acknowledge I was actually losing my sight, though not a single one of us mentioned the B-word.

Given the intensity of the pandemic, Hayden turned to unhealthy choices to handle his distress, while Stew got busy picking up the slack of our household—without complaint and even more so with a compliance I had never seen in his approach to managing our home. I was astounded and grateful we could keep functioning as normally as we had prior to my diagnosis. When people brought us food, Stew immediately followed with hand-written thank you notes, stuffed with little chocolates, when he had not written a thank you note in years. He never told me. He just did it. I found out from one of our friends who said, "He didn't have to send us a note." I had no control. Stew took over.

Mackenzie helped Stew with other household tasks but she was also in college and finishing her bachelor's degree. She was there for me and her brothers emotionally, taking on the role, unknowingly, of playing the family therapist and mom. They confided in her when they didn't feel they could talk to me about the situation. She often visited me at the hospital in Stanford and treated me normally, offering compassion, while her brothers and dad shut down. It was understandable. They were terrified of losing me more than acknowledging I was losing my sight. The painful and alienating truth was that my family struggled to feel normal around me.

Grady was a tougher nut to crack. He was angry and pissed that this had happened to me. He had just become a teenager and had no idea how to handle the tsunami of emotion that washed up on his childhood shore and beat him sideways. His response was to shut down, too. Every one of my family members wanted to love me, but underneath all their anxiety was such loss. I didn't know how much loss they were experiencing. I was so overwhelmed with the minute by minute of my condition, I had no idea how much their lives were also changing as a result.

Everything was not fine. I had lost control. I had lost my freedom. I could not do the things I used to do without even thinking about it. Like walking out of my door by myself. Walking, period. Going to the gym alone. Driving to the store to get groceries or even buying groceries because, let's face it, I could no longer see the shelves, let alone try to purchase anything online, including clothes, which I could not see on a screen or a rack in the store. It was all mounting. Day after day. The little things I once took for granted started to top my wishlist of the things I wanted to do again, by myself, with two good eyes. Or even one good eye. Or even a half of a good eye.

I wanted to see the world and navigate it like I was used to, but the Universe had other plans. The worst was that I could not drive and had to surrender my super-sweet Audi Q5. It made no sense to keep paying for a car I would no longer be driving. I would have to rely on family members, friends, or Uber and found myself so frustrated I could not just take off whenever and wherever I wanted to go. I felt trapped.

Still, the most devastating experience for me was not being able to look into my family's eyes. My kids and husband were so good about keeping things real with me and still allowing me to hold their faces in my hands and get up close enough that I could look through the veil and try to see how they had changed, grown, and continued to be my sweet babies. Complicating things, I could no longer see the photos of them and others I loved on my phone and had to rely on my memory. I would also miss seeing the big events and began to ask friends and family to document them for me.

While I navigated all of this, I also kept reminding myself to not worry and just be present. This was a great theory. I wanted to trust in its power to deliver me from this hell, but I was still waging a battle within myself that would not end anytime soon. I was struggling on a daily basis to keep my shit together. I wanted to scream every day that everything was not fine. I wanted to scream that I was so mad about being in this situation and why the hell did this have to happen to me? I wanted to scream at God and tell him that this joke he was playing on me was messed up and no one deserved it.

My mind went in circles. I wondered if I'd done something in a past life to make me deserve living like this. If I had, I offered atonement. Asked for forgiveness. Prayed for miracles. I wanted my eyesight to be restored in all its glory. I wanted to snap my fingers and restore my dignity and daily routine. I wish I could tell you that's what happened.

In fact, something was working through me. Each day as I threw my inner tantrums while still plastering a smile on my face and forcing a cheery tone in my voice, telling people "I'm fine! Everything's under control, folks," something gave way.

I noticed a very small shift in my perspective. It slowly occurred to me that maybe this experience was actually not about me.

I had taken everything so personally. But what if it wasn't personal?

What if this was a collective mission?

What if this was not happening to me but *for me*?

I wrestled with these thoughts, calling bullshit half the time. The other half I found myself leaning into what was being spoken to me—through others and the world. I told my friend Sarah that maybe I should be grateful this was happening because otherwise I would not have met others who helped me find a new path.

Sarah saw it a little bit differently. "The Universe took you out with a two-by-four and if it wasn't this, your eyesight and gut being what took you out, it would have been something else, maybe worse."

"What could be worse than this?" I asked.

This was my worst-case scenario, which I have come to realize is different for everyone. For others it might be hearing loss, stroke, being paralyzed, having cancer... the list goes on and on. As angry as I was, I explained I had also discovered the opposite of my anger was pure love. I had suddenly acknowledged my paradox.

I was grateful for those who had shown up for me to read me the menu at the restaurant that they drove me to, for my family and friends who were there for me during the messy moments of my recovery and sad moments. I was grateful for the strangers who saw me standing in the public bathroom at the airport, with its super bright fluorescent lights, and asked me if I needed help finding an open bathroom stall.

And while everything was not fine in my head, I was starting to move toward a more comprehensive understanding in the midst of my despair. That, in fact, I was not being punished. I had done nothing wrong. I was just experiencing the expansiveness of the human condition, even when it sucked donkey balls, as the saying goes.

Over the coming days and weeks, I began to experience a feeling of pure love for the angels both in spirit and in human form who came to guide me in the direction of what my life would look like by pouring my story into a book and sharing this crazy, effed-up, beautiful, blessed, and messy journey I am working my way through.

I realized that maybe it was true after all. Everything might actually be fine... someday. Either way, I knew this much to be true: the love surrounding me was so much stronger than my anger. This beautiful mess of my life was worth wherever it was leading me.

CHAPTER 11

INTO THE WOO-WOO WE GO

HAVING ENTERED THE PORTAL to discover how to heal my visual impairment and, more importantly, my body and spirit, I discovered new ways to tap into my past trauma. While meeting the shaman in Big Sur was the beginning of a journey into looking outside the box of those who might be able to help me, when I began to engage with psychics, mediums, and therapists, the world of alternative medicine shifted my life once again.

I was open, willing, and ready to heal by *any* means. While I was still going to acupuncture, craniosacral therapy, and energy healing, I was introduced to a few other facets of integrative medicine. When a close friend asked if I would be interested in a kambo ceremony, I said, "Yes!" Why not, right? I had no idea what the hell kambo was (it's a poison used as a traditional medicine in purging or cleansing rituals, primarily in South America. It is a waxy substance collected by scraping the skin of an Amazon tree frog, *Phyllomedusa bicolor*), but without hesitation, I asked, "When is it and what time do I need to be ready?"

Since we were late for the sign up and unable to meet with the facilitator, we had to wing it and just show up, totally unprepared, for the four-hour ceremony. We received only an email with a brief explanation of what kambo was and what to expect. Because I couldn't see, I didn't read the email, of course, but asked my friend to read it to me the day before the ceremony. She laughed after finishing the email. "Holy shit!" she said. "You will most likely puke or shit yourself during the ceremony."

I stiffened, thinking this was not funny. I couldn't see. I didn't want to shit myself or puke in public, but I was committed and, the next afternoon, hopped into her car to experience an afternoon of kambo, with the distant fear of public defecation. We hit traffic on the way to the ceremony and arrived a few minutes late, putting us behind the eight ball already, which did nothing to boost my confidence in this decision.

Despite our tardy arrival, the ceremony hadn't started, thankfully. I noticed three other participants sitting in the room, which forced me and my friend to split up. Despite my growing hesitation about this shit-yourself gathering, I still had great hope kambo might restore my eyesight. I was okay with the seating arrangement but quietly mentioned to the facilitator that I had a vision issue and might need a little help. She understood and offered assistance if I needed it. I took my seat to the left of her, sitting criss-cross applesauce, back straight, and ready to learn about what the hell I had signed up for here.

On my left sat a very nice gentleman (the only guy participating in the ceremony), there was a gal to his left, my friend next to her (diagonal from me), and then directly across from me sat the last gal, making five of us. Music was playing while the facilitator waved burning sage to clear the air and space before the ceremony. I liked the music—a bit like angelic pop—and found it soothing, which made me want to dance.

Once everyone was done getting saged the facilitator asked if any of us had our own pipes to take in a snuff of pure tobacco. Having been late to the details, I didn't read this and had no idea what she was talking about, but two of the other participants whipped out their pipes, as if she'd asked them to present their yoga mats, and immediately filled them with tobacco. The facilitator allowed me and my friend to use her pipe. The man to my left passed on the offer, sharing that he was a recovering addict. *Okay, then. Thank you for sharing,* I thought, wondering about the constellation of derelicts, misfits, and desperate folks like me who had gathered for this ceremony. Because of my placement in the room, I was unfortunately the last participant to receive the "medicine." With that being said, I could see where everyone was placed in the room, just not the details of facial expressions or anything else happening due to the veil covering my vision. But I could hear the angelic pop music playing while my friend received her intake of pure tobacco.

The facilitator was whispering to each participant as she approached them but I wasn't able to hear her. What I did hear was my friend pseudo-inhale the pipe and say, "Holy crap, that burns a little and my eyes are watering!" *What? Oh no.* Of course, the first thing that ran through my mind were flashbacks of being in high school and getting a throat burn after smoking pot out of a bong. I laughed to myself remembering those days, thankful I had some experience with inhaling plant-based medicine. I wasn't totally new to this rodeo, I believed. I could handle this, right?

SHOULD'VE SEEN THAT COMING

When it was finally my turn to take in the sacred tobacco, I felt nervous but excited to do it, thinking the entire time, *This is part of the formula to restore my vision! Smoke up, Jamie!* I was no longer questioning inhaling the Irish weed at this point; I was finally surrendering to any type of alternative medicine that had the potential to heal my eyes. When the facilitator sat in front of me, she quietly whispered to me not to inhale the tobacco when taking it in. This was profoundly odd to me. How could I or anyone not do that? She explained I would pull in the smoke but not let it into my lungs, then exhale out my mouth. At first, I wondered if this was a trick of coordination, similar to patting your head and rubbing your tummy at the same time. Not easy. When I mentioned this, hoping she might laugh, she was silent. I realized this was serious stuff and my teenage self would have no power to control anything now by being a goofball. When the pipe was ready, I opened my mouth and reached for it. The facilitator said she would hold it for me, but instead of placing the end of the pipe in my mouth, she placed it in my left nostril. Needless to say, I was a bit taken back but did exactly what she said to do.

What I wasn't expecting was her blowing into the other end of the pipe, which pushed what felt like a small kernel up into my nose. Once I exhaled the smoke out through my mouth she proceeded to place the pipe in my right nostril and blow another kernel up into my nose. Both of my eyes were watering, and I thought, *Maybe this will help clear all of the shit out of my eyes and allow me to see again.*

After everyone was full of the clearing tobacco (with the exception of the recovering addict to my left), the facilitator explained what would happen next. We were to embark on the actual meat of the ceremony. She explained that kambo is basically derived from a poisonous frog from the Amazon. This type of frog has powers in its poison that is excreted from its back. The natives lick the frog's back to ingest the poison and subsequently purge any toxins that might be making them sick. I sat up. This was not in the email literature that my friend read to me yesterday. As I listened to the explanation, I found myself battling this part of the process. *There is no way I am going to lick a frog*, I thought. I had reached my edge.

She continued to explain the process. To my great relief, there would be no frogs to lick today; however, to get the frog poison effectively into our bodies we would have to be branded with three burn holes where she would administer the poison. I sat up straight, reconsidering her words. No joke. We were about to get burned.

Because I was last in line, I was able to focus on listening to the nature soundtrack she was now playing while she branded the rest of our group. I was having grave misgivings while I sat there and swore I heard the sizzle of burning flesh. What was I doing? Nobody told me about the branding part, but it was too late to hightail it out of there. I just sat listening to the searing of skin as the facilitator made her rounds on each of us in the circle. When it was finally my turn, I chose to have the burn holes placed on the outside of my right arm—and figured this was akin to a burn tattoo, which would have been my first—and soon last. For the first time since I had lost my sight, not being able to see details was a blessing.

Each burn hole was done with a charred piece of wood about the size of a fat marker; it felt a lot like a yellow jacket sting. I assumed at the time that she was not only putting on the burn holes but also administering the frog poison.

After she finished, I sat there ready for the poison to do what I had hoped—cure me immediately, restore my central vision. Call this a day and move on. I was expecting the poison to kick in and for me to feel strange or sick, but that is not what happened. Turns out at that point I had only received the burn holes—the frog poison was yet to be administered.

I sat there watching the facilitator move on to the gal directly across from me. I thought for a few minutes that they must be friends because they were chatting to themselves and I couldn't see what was happening. While waiting for my turn to receive the dose of the frog poison, I did a quick inventory of what was around me: blanket, mat, pillow and puke bucket. Then all of a sudden I heard a horrible noise. The noise every human dreads be it from their sick child or wildly drunk friend. The girl began puking her guts out. Thoughts were running like wildfire through my mind. *Oh hell, no! I had better not throw up when I catch a whiff of her vomit.* Then I wondered, *How is no one else vomiting?* Then suddenly I wondered if it would be bad if I burst out laughing. Poor gal. She sounded wretched. I just wanted to give her a hug. I noticed the facilitator spraying some type of neutralizing spray, feeling sorry for my friend who was sitting beside Puker.

We sat and listened to Puker filling the bucket a few times for nearly five minutes. I felt like a voyeur. Now it was my friend's turn and I was anticipating another round of puke while the other gal drifted off to sleep. I heard my friend gag over her bucket and then she got up and ran to the bathroom. I was now panicking. I was certain that she was not only going to puke but also shit her pants. My mind raced. *Oh, no!* I thought. *What if I shit my pants, too?* I hadn't brought an extra pair of pants (there was no checklist and besides, we hadn't read the fine print) and suddenly imagined myself riding home with a blanket (that I would have stolen from the studio) to cover my naked lower half.

A few minutes later, my friend returned wearing her same jeans and no smell of poop. She had finished her puking, politely in the privacy of the bathroom, thank God. Now it was time for the gal seated between my friend and the dude next to me. She was by far my favorite participant. She was so vocal and didn't hold anything back. It's like I was experiencing a form of surreal entertainment as I smiled and laughed to myself. I was able to catch a little more of what the facilitator was instructing her about with what was going to happen. The kambo ceremony evidently wasn't her first rodeo. She had burn holes in a few spots on her body. Could she be a kambo junkie? Either way, I sent her love and hoped for the best. For all of our sakes.

While I was anticipating the puke fest to continue as Girl 3 received her first dose of the frog poison, the dude next to me whispered, "The anticipation is killing me!" I told him I couldn't agree more: "This waiting is definitely not mentioned in the brochure." He laughed quietly as we continued to sit there listening to the sound of frogs of the Amazon singing their songs while hopefully muffling the puke sounds.

Unfortunately Girl 3's purging was epic. She was the most vocal. While she hit her puke bucket like a champ, I was also tripping out at the dude, who was suddenly guzzling so much water you would have thought he had been walking through the Sahara Desert for days. I thought to myself, *This guy is going to throw all of that water up. What the hell is he thinking?* Meanwhile, Girl 3 had stopped vomiting but was sobbing. Not any sob, but an all-out guttural anguish. And then, to my utter consternation, she started to make a breathy sound that sounded a lot like an orgasm. I sent her love. While all of this was happening, my friend was laughing her ass off because she said that my head turned toward the direction of Girl 3 with a WTF look. I didn't find it funny. I was horrified wondering if I, too, might have an orgasm next to the water guzzler.

Once Girl 3 was done with her orgasmic puke sob, the facilitator administered the frog poison to the dude sitting just a foot away from me. I had to endure him puking into his bucket and purging all of his junkie toxins. All I could do was turn away to avoid smelling him. But I also sent him love, because guess what, it was now my turn for the main medicine of this ceremony.

The facilitator knelt in front of me. Music played from her cell phone, attached to a holster at her side. She smiled when I told her, "Let's just get this done."

She placed a drop of frog poison into the first burn hole. Once the drop was placed I sat there waiting to feel something. A few minutes went by and I was feeling good. Everyone else was resting quietly and I wondered if this would have a different effect on me. Or any effect at all. Considering all of the trauma my gut had already been through, I imagined it cursing at me saying, "Really, Jamie, don't you think we have been through enough?" My response was, yes, we have, but let's try this anyway.

Just as I got done having the discussion with my gut, the facilitator was in front of me, asking in the voice of a concerned parent, "How are you feeling?" My answer came out a little more perky than I expected, "I am good!" To my surprise, I felt great—no nausea—and I was feeling like maybe I was going to be immune to this plant medicine due to all of the man-made drugs I'd had while I was in the hospital. Before I knew it, the facilitator was placing another drop of frog poison into my second burn hole.

I sat there waiting for my gut to start to growl and gurgle, warning me that she was going to blow. The facilitator returned to me after checking on the others who were all sleeping by now. She asked me if I was nauseous and my response was, again in the perky and I am sure annoying voice, "No, I am good." I wore a shit-eating grin, thinking I was going to dodge a vomit bullet and leave high on pure tobacco and frog poison. She then asked me, "Have you drunk any of your water?" I said, "Yes, a little." She now had the look and response of a parent who is ready to give you a big, fat lecture and instructed me to drink the entire large bottle of water after she gave me the rest of the poison.

She proceeded to give me another drop of frog poison into the third burn hole. Once that was done, I obediently drank the contents of my bottle as she watched me like a hawk. By the time I was done drinking the second bottle of water my body slowly started to put up its middle finger. I had the puke bucket in place and gagged a few times to no avail. Instead, I felt like I was going to pass out. The facilitator was there to help me lay down and, of course, the second my head hit the pillow I reached for the puke bucket and my body laughed while she snorted, "There she blows!"

Once all of the water was out of me, I laid down and snuggled up on my mat with my blanket ready for a restful nap like everyone else, but five minutes later the facilitator woke everyone up. "Okay, let's start getting ready to close out the ceremony." I thought, *Are you fucking kidding me? I only got a five-minute rest and Puker 1 has been snoring and restfully sleeping for the last two hours.*

Being kambo compliant, I rose from my five-minute cat nap and sat criss-cross applesauce again. The facilitator made closing comments, which I only half heard with three drops of frog poison still coursing through my system, while I tried to clamp down on a fart that was working its way out of my bottom. I clenched, trying to hold it in, when Girl 3 asked very loudly, "Do you have any dragon's blood?" My ears perked up and I turned her direction. The facilitator said she had some but that it wouldn't do anything for you except make you look cool. The girl insisted, imploring her to use it to help the sting from the burn holes. The facilitator complied and then asked the rest of the group if we'd like some dragon's blood (as much as I wished this was the blood of a real dragon, the facilitator explained to us that it was simply a plant-based red resin) to ease the burns. I shot my hand up so fast I almost threw my shoulder out of its socket, and I felt my fart go. When the facilitator approached me with it, I told her, "I don't care if it helps; I just want to look cool."

***

I left the kambo experience with no change in my vision and decided to pause from any other plant-based ceremonies so my body didn't totally revolt. Five months later, my kambo friend invited me to a breathwork and mushroom microdosing ceremony at the same studio, and I couldn't resist. While I was feeding my fantasy that maybe this ceremony would restore my eyesight, I embarked with a little more savvy about plant-based medicine and had done more homework. And I had a lot more hope that this would restore my eyesight.

For weeks leading up to this event, I did daily tests to measure what I could see and could not see. I would close my right eye and keep my left eye open to focus on whatever I could. Usually it was dark in the left eye, but I could still see the shapes of things and some light through the muted darkness. A part of me wanted to believe that others understood what I was seeing or how it looked to me.

Determined to fight the lazy eye I felt emerging there, I would move my left eyeball around as if I was warming up an ankle to prepare to run.

I would do the same test by covering my left eye and keeping my right eye open, which was the eye I could still see light through, including peripheral vision. It was like looking through a dirty window. I could see, just not well. For example, I could tell if someone was wearing a hat or glasses, if they had jeans or slacks, a skirt or handbag. I could see and sense objects but without any of the details. People started to compliment me on how bright both my eyes looked. I have big turquoise-blue eyes, accentuated by my blond hair, but I had never heard this many people tell me how bright they looked. These daily tests and odd compliments were a measure of how my sight was staying the same. It was like a tease. I say all of this because I felt like my inner light was able to see for me, though at the time, I was unable to articulate this when it was all so new. Despite this ability to see through the darkness, I was desperate to restore my central vision and restore the screen, so to speak. I wanted everything to go back to "normal" and, God willing, had faith that some magic mushrooms would do the trick. Giddy up.

This time, I entered the ceremony space with more confidence and a twinge of cockiness. It was my way of not letting my mind take over and question my decision to try mushrooms—in my early fifties. In this ceremony there were about fifteen participants with mostly women and a few men. I soon learned I was the second oldest person there and assumed this was the thing the kids were doing so I'd take one for the middle-aged team and be the test dummy for everyone on the fence about microdosing.

Although I could not see the participants' faces, we got comfortable on our yoga mats, with blankets and pillows at the ready. The facilitator was a young gal who I sensed was in her twenties. She had a sweet voice and made me feel so warm and fuzzy inside as she explained how the evening would go. We would be given a yummy iced tea to drink with a twinge of hibiscus and a solid dose of "shrooms."

She said we might want to take our time drinking the mixture so we didn't peak too soon during the evening. Although I wanted to down that delicious cup of iced tea, I nursed it slowly, wanting to have the full experience of this particular ceremony. As we finished up drinking our "shroom" libations, we were asked to then relax onto our yoga mats with our pillow behind our heads and our blanket over us.

I felt like I was at nap time in preschool. She instructed us to take some deep breaths—in through the nose and out through the mouth for about five minutes. Then we began a form of holotropic breathwork, inhaling and exhaling with more vigor. I felt like I was panting. The sweet young woman said to the group that if anyone needed to make sounds during the breathwork, they were more than welcome to let it out. By this time, everyone in the room was breathing heavily, which sounded a lot like orgasmic gasps.

I hoped nobody had COVID-19. No one was wearing a mask and we were spewing heavy breaths into the air. Just as I started to get a little worried, I suddenly felt relaxed and no longer concerned if anyone's spittle landed on my face. Oh, boy. The mushrooms had kicked in, and I found myself in a happy and calm place. It was so different from marijuana. It didn't make me tired, lazy, or super hungry. Just relaxed and happy.

While we were laying on our mats, the young facilitator played some background music, including a range of acoustic guitar, instrumental, and African and Australian aboriginal tunes. I was the most relaxed I had been in a long time. Then the facilitator started to play a didgeridoo, pushing the sound through her lips to produce a continuous deep-throated sound while using circular breathing to keep it going. She was playing so strongly and at one point walked over and aimed it at my face. I felt the deep vibrations of the didgeridoo pulsing over my face, hoping that my eyesight would clear because the mushrooms would have done their magic.

What happened instead was that my body started to involuntarily move—similar to when I would twitch on the table during my craniosacral therapy appointments, except this time my body was moving to the music. I was grateful that everyone was laying down and had their eyes closed. I didn't want anyone to think I was having a seizure or that a demonic presence had suddenly possessed me. I was simply feeling happy and light.

After about an hour of music, body dancing, flailing, heavy breathing, and microdosing we sat up and said a meditation to close out the ceremony. The facilitator then brought out snacks and although I didn't think I was hungry I threw down a few mini muffins and a handful of popcorn. When saying our goodbyes to the class and facilitator, the facilitator said, "Wow, Jamie, you were really into the ceremony tonight."

I told her, "You gave a great symphony and ceremony, thank you!"

Despite how great I felt, I left the studio with the veil still over my eyes. The mushrooms hadn't brought me on any wild trip. I had no hallucinations. I had not barfed. I had not lost anything other than a belief that was no longer serving me—that I could restore my central vision. But for the first time I had let go and felt happy. Maybe that was the point? Maybe that was the magic mushrooms at work after all? The experience helped me realize just how much I had been expanding my life because of my disability, and this accelerated growth was helping me see things differently. I was seeing what I had never seen before and beginning to appreciate this new point of view.

CHAPTER 12

BELLY OF THE BEAST

WHILE SECRETS TO MY HEALING had been unlocked, I knew I had more work to do. I understood that other forces were working to protect me but had forgotten this over the years and struggled so many times when I felt sad and scared, feeling like the world was closing in on me. During the first two years of my diagnosis, I continued to live this paradox, feeling divinely guided while also doubting any kind of support at all. This vicious cycle prevented me from progressing—tied to past trauma that had been retriggered by the diagnosis. I felt stuck. Unhappy. Frustrated and pissed.

I found myself dwelling on what I had lost, what I could not do, while also trying to appear upbeat, positive, and grateful for what I did have and what I still could do. I would be up one day, feeling the support, then down the next, feeling alone and terrified by all the uncertainty and unanswered questions, desperate for my central eyesight to return. I yo-yoed like this for nearly three years, doing the dance between trust and doubt. I hated it and I wanted out. But it would take more uncovering the beast that still lurked within to identify the trigger of this trauma and stop the loop that caused me so much suffering.

Recalling that the ancestral clearing work was helping me get to the root of my belly issue, a vivid memory surfaced during this deep dive into the memory bank. I was ten, living in a house I really liked because I loved climbing the big maple tree in the backyard. We were still living in Kansas but had moved three times in two years into a neighborhood I wasn't familiar with and where I had no friends.

I was in fifth grade, trying to find my voice, which included cuss words—perhaps to fit in. I felt like I had to confess to my mom about how much I was cursing at school with my friends but not in front of the teachers or adults. One day, I came home from school and announced, "Mom, I have to tell you something and I am afraid to tell you."

She stared at me with a poker face. "If you are being honest about something then you won't get into trouble. What is it that you need to tell me?"

I wasn't sure how to read her face and wondered what she was thinking. *Was she serious? I wouldn't get into trouble for cussing?* I took a deep breath and confessed.

"I have been cussing a lot at school."

My mom sat back in her chair at the kitchen table and studied me for a moment.

"What types of cuss words are you saying, Jamie?"

I blinked back the tears forming and blurted, "Shit, fuck, damn, and bastard."

I was so nervous that she was going to be so mad and ground me.

She drew in a breath and her lips formed a little pout. My heart pounded.

Finally, she spoke, "Do you know what a bastard is?"

I felt my eyes bug out. My mom had just said *bastard!*

"No," I told her. I had no idea what a bastard was.

What she told me next would alter the course of the rest of my life.

"Well, *you* are a bastard."

The word landed on me like a wad of phlegm, even though I still had no idea what it meant. I could just feel that something had gone terribly wrong—far worse than my imagined repercussions of confessing my playground potty mouth. My mom fixed her eyes on my face, which must have been priceless.

She explained, "A bastard is when a child doesn't have a father."

What? I stared at her, trying to make sense of this but feeling like we'd just cracked a dozen eggs and could do nothing about all the whites dripping all over the place. Nothing would ever go back together the same for me after this moment.

A bastard is when a child doesn't have a father.

She fired out the words, blunt and to the point. It would take another three years for her to disclose that I actually had a father, then forty more years for the full story to understand the hostility in her voice. She was a young, single mother working three jobs to support two children. She was doing everything she could to keep us safe and secure, even though she did not feel that most of the time herself. If epigenetics is true, then it was a natural inheritance for me—this lifelong struggle with feeling safe; however, all that time we had angels with us while we were growing up together.

Perhaps it was under these conditions that my intuition became one of my super powers at such a young age. In the midst of this experience of ancestral clearing, I recounted another memory when I was ten that would identify yet another mass of calcified energy stuck in my gut. My sister, Sara, and I were home alone for a few hours before my mom returned home from work. Our phone was disconnected again because we didn't have the money to pay the bill so Sara and I walked to the grocery store a few blocks from our house to use the payphone to call Mom and let her know we made it home safe and sound from school. While we were walking home, I could sense that something was wrong. We were only a block away from our house when I noticed a guy driving slowly down our street and instinctively knew he was up to no good. At the time, I didn't think that maybe he was just looking for the address of a friend. And remember, DoorDash and Uber didn't exist during the late '70s. There were no deliveries or pick-ups other than from taxi drivers, which were all identified. The guy was suspicious. I told Sara, "Let's pretend that this house is ours so that this creeper doesn't know where we live."

Sara was confused. She was only five years old. She didn't understand what I wanted her to do and why. But she always trusted me as her big sister.

"Creeper?" she asked in her tiny voice.

"I think that's a Bad Guy," I said and started toward the neighbor's house.

She listened, and we acted like the neighbor's house was ours. The guy drove by and once he was out of sight we sprinted to our house, which was still a block away.

We weren't safe yet. I saw the guy come around again, certain he was looking for us, and I made Sara duck behind some hedges and stay still. After he passed, not seeing us, we got up and ran to our house. We were shaking with fear and our hearts were pounding. Sara clutched my hand and we finally made it into the house.

"Get down!" I told her as soon as we got inside and closed the door.

"Why?" she screamed, panicked.

"He might see us!" I said as I fumbled with the lock.

We had a big picture window in the front room, without shades or curtains, which weren't in my mom's budget, so we army crawled across the floor so that if the Bad Guy drove by again he would not know where we lived.

We laid like this for almost three hours until my mom got home. Two sisters, clutching each other, terrified they were going to get kidnapped. That kind of trauma remains in the body if it's not released. The cortisol and adrenaline rushed through our bodies, readying us to fly, freeze, or fight. We knew we would stand no chance if the Bad Guy came to get us. Those three hours seemed like an eternity and, in a way, they were. That memory was imprinted in my stomach for four decades and is no doubt one of the leading causes of the inflammation causing the diverticulitis. While this made perfect sense to me, I was astounded that no other doctor would have asked me about my past to discover what John Newton did to link my trauma to my dis-ease. No, *dis-ease* is not a typo. As the late author Louise Hay put it, *dis-ease* is the way your body experiences pain, with the pain or discomfort being caused by emotions you hold within your body.

When my mom got home that evening, we told her about what happened. I just remember the look on her face—complete and utter horror. She pressed us both against her and I still remember feeling the wetness of her tears through my T-shirt. She said little but acted quickly and shortly after, we ended up moving to a different town and living with my aunt, uncle, and their three young kids. While we were on a mission to move on from our past, it would continue to follow and haunt us until we were both strong enough to confront it and she would reveal who my real father was. Still, connecting these two stories now, it was evident we'd had no male figures in our lives on a daily basis to make us feel safe. My belly could hold a lot, I would soon learn, for better or for worse, and I was on a dangerous path to test its capacity.

***

The ancestral clearing work that I did with John, and subsequently with my friend Sarah, was catalyzing my first spirit growth after my vision loss. By tapping into eight-year-old Jamie, he helped me identify the times when she felt scared and abandoned—without the presence or protection of the Divine Masculine in my life. His method was extraordinary. He pulled out memories I had buried so damn deep that I completely forgot about them until that moment. With his loving guidance, I allowed my subconscious to speak her truth, and holy shit, she had a lot to say.

A question that came to me in my ancestral clearing work had me recall a time in my life when I saw something I didn't particularly want to see. Maybe a time when I turned a blind eye to something happening right in front of me. Or was there a specific trauma I'd endured? The question was asked, Were you a certain age that you can recall any or all of these things happening?

I felt safe enough to allow my subconscious to speak her truth. I recalled when I was fourteen and with a guy I really liked. We were on a date and parked at a known makeout spot in San Diego, which is where I lived at the time. Although I was only fourteen, I had plenty of practice making out with boys, so I wasn't opposed to that part of the date. What happened after that was when I went into the freeze mode of the fight, flight, or freeze. John asked, "What happened that night with that boy?"

I explained everything was going great with the date until he wanted to do more than I wanted to sexually. I was still a virgin and wasn't ready to have sex with a guy who I had only gone on one or two dates with. But the guy pushed and tried to touch me in my private parts that I didn't want him to touch. When I told him no, he said yes. I again repeated that I didn't want him to touch me there but he persisted. Thinking I was smart, I told him I was on my period. You would think that would have been it, but he said, "No, you aren't," and proceeded to check by putting his fingers and hands in the one place I held sacred and that was mine to give, not his to take.

Once he was satisfied I wasn't on my period, he proceeded to do whatever he wanted. I lay frozen and felt as if I'd left my body. In fact I had. This is known as disassociation and when people say, "She was beside herself," they mean just that. It is not a turn of phrase. It is a literal saying that my spirit had left my body in order for it to survive this trauma. And I didn't know how to reconcile with this, who to tell, or what to do when it was happening. I went quiet. Once he was done, he drove me home and I vowed to never talk with or see this asshole ever again.

But as my subconscious revealed this memory, I remembered that I lasted about six months before reconnecting with this boy, and this time I was lured again by his charm and ended up letting him do more than just get to third base. He was my first consensual sexual experience and we dated for about a year. I ended up falling in love with him and he floated in and out of my life, even after we broke up when I was sixteen. We were linked energetically and it never felt good the older I got. What I would learn later is that this boy's violation of me was so deep that what I had truly experienced is something I can only explain as a physical and energetic assault on my body and soul. It would take me decades to uncover this trauma.

I finally broke away from this boy when I was in my mid twenties. Once I shared this experience with John, he asked, "What would you say to your fourteen-year-old self about this situation?" My response to her was, "How could you be so stupid?!"

I carried so much shame around this incident, having no idea how destructive it was. I had blamed myself for years, thinking I had done something wrong. But it was not my fault. I had said no. Over and over. Realizing this, I let out a huge exhale.

I was finally able to breathe into that acknowledgement and receive a clearing. It was such a blessing to take a full, deep breath, filling my lungs and belly fully for the first time in nearly forty years and seeing how this event had weighed me down for most of my life. It was never my fault. I was only fourteen years old and didn't have the maturity and strength to stand my ground, get out of the car, and go home. My body froze. I left it. I know that I am not alone with unfortunate events like this happening and that women and girls are sexually assaulted every minute of every day. Tragically, we hold this life event within our bodies, letting it eat away at the bright light we are.

I can honestly say at this point that I feel as if I have released the shame, guilt, and anger over that event in my life. The light inside me is not as dim now. After that potent clearing with John, he asked me to imagine myself standing outside the car, as my fourteen-year-old self. Kneeling before me is Jesus, placing his hands over my eyes, helping me heal from this traumatic event. He also said that standing behind me was the Divine Feminine, Mother Mary, and that she had my back and would always be there to comfort and hold me.

While we worked on this, I felt something I had never experienced in my life. At that moment when John mentioned Mother Mary, I swear I could feel her clothing when she embraced me. I was filled with so much love and grace. I was also filled with sorrow for all that was stolen from me but restored in that moment. It was one of the most beautiful moments of my healing journey.

I would realize later that the Divine Feminine, God, and Jesus have been with me all along. They were telling me that in order to truly heal, not just my eyesight and gut but my whole person, I had to do the deep dive into the sludge that keeps me stuck in a lower vibration, or a place where I easily self-deprecate and abandon my self-love. I know I am capable of raising my vibration so I can heal and see my life clearly, both spiritually and physically. If you are reading this and feel buried by your own trauma, I know you can also raise your vibration. If I can do it, you can, too. It is not a solo event. You are surrounded by so much spiritual support that healing is inevitable—if you allow it.

The many spiritual and energetic modalities I was exploring had awakened my past so I could heal my present. Clearly the ancestral healing he performed was straightening up any outdated agreements I had with anyone in my family lineage. It was like performing housekeeping on epigenetics. Some stuff needed to go to the great Goodwill of the spirit world. I was ready to let go of anything that was cluttering my energetic space if it meant I could heal, and I was beginning to sense that healing might look different than I imagined. While my initial goal was to regain my central vision, I was starting to sense it wasn't the vision that I was to regain but other gifts and opportunities to let go and grow instead.

CHAPTER 13

A NEW COMPASS

OVER THE YEARS, I WAS slowly being led to others who were showing me alternative methods of developing my spirituality—which would serve me decades later to deal with my new capacity to see eyes and spirits—without my central vision. While I had struggled to find a true spiritual connection in my life, a spirit was guiding me to other paths that would help me gain a larger understanding of being a spirit in a human body and feeling supported by angels.

Three years after breaking up with the boy who left a metaphorical bruise on my heart and soul, I started dating a guy I knew in high school. I was nineteen and much more aware of my body, my sexuality, and how to navigate being with a boy. Marc was funny, sweet, and we always had fun together. He was my first safe male. When he introduced me to his parents, I immediately connected with his mom, Judy, who would initiate me into the next level of my spirituality.

I felt a beautiful connection to her immediately and remember visiting their house one evening when she told me that their dog had been acting strange lately but they figured out the cause. Without hesitation or wondering what I might think, she explained there was a spirit living in one of the bedrooms. While I had never had an experience with a spirit or ghost like that at the time, I remember being impressed that she would share this so openly, but even more so that she felt comfortable sharing it with me. She was so matter of fact that it helped me open up to what she shared next. Apparently, a clairvoyant friend of hers had also come over to the house to help the spirit cross over from this realm to the next. The dog was acting strangely because the spirit was disgruntled existing between the realms. She went on to explain the process to me as if I was a longtime believer in the metaphysical and spiritual world.

I was beside myself. I had never met anyone like her. Nobody talked about these things, and the mention of them felt oddly familiar and restorative, like a language I had not heard in years and did not realize I already had fluency in. I was astounded by what she was bringing up for me, just three years after this incident with the boy I still carried, suppressing all the trauma as deep as I could into the darkest bowels of my belly.

Not that he was a ghost. Or an entity. But that his presence had lingered, as if our interaction together had imprinted me. So in a way, yes, I was still carrying the ghost of our relationship, which had ended years ago but was somehow still burdening my body. Nobody had ever connected the dots for me until Judy.

How did she know I needed to hear about all of this now? I knew instantly that Judy would be a teacher for the rest of my life. She introduced me to meditation, crystals, and the power and energy they hold—preparing me for my journey into the woo-woo decades later. She was my safe space to be my true self and never made me feel like I was crazy when asking her questions about the metaphysical world.

A few years later, when I was twenty-three, I experienced my first psychic reading by a woman who looked like she could be anyone's grandma. Her name was June Siebur, and it was 1993—long before smart phones, internet, or anything digital where someone like her could quickly look up facts and figures about me and perform a circus trick with her mind. June was the real deal. My friend Anna was in the room with me during the reading so she could take notes because we were not allowed to use a tape recorder. Not because June prohibited them, but because in her experience the recordings only ended up sounding like static.

Anna and I looked at each other with wide eyes. Was she serious? We both had chills. Truth be known, we were a little spooked. Who wouldn't be, right? First time with a psychic. We had no idea what to expect. My mind was wide open and I was ready to hear what my future held. Would she whip out a crystal ball and fill the room with fog? Not at all. She said a prayer to set an intention, acknowledging guidance from God, the four winds, and the spirits of the Native Americans who would guide her and me during the reading. The whole reading was fascinating.

She saw I would live amongst a lot of trees and that I had a red flag over my head, which meant success. She also saw my three spirit guides, mentioned I would meet a man with dark hair and light eyes, have three kids with him— specifically one girl and two boys—and she saw that I would be helping people by teaching them something about their past. This was strikingly accurate. I married dark-haired, blue-eyed Stew. We had three kids, a daughter and two sons. We live in a forested neighborhood, and I am now on a path of spiritual teaching. That wasn't a bad set of details for a twenty-three year old.

This was another confirmation I was meant to learn more about this world of woo-woo. Over the next thirty years, it made me more aware of signs from my guides and angels. I started to appreciate the small and significant events that would happen in my life—everything from chance encounters with people to meaningful gatherings like that in the barn where I met the Rose Girls. Eventually, I started to see the Divine Design between the entire network of people who had shown up in my life over the years and I could better appreciate their role, even if we'd only interacted a few times.

Although I was intrigued by the metaphysical and spiritual world, my focus shifted to other interests as I got older. Instead of expanding my spiritual awareness, I put a cap on it and spent the next twenty-three years living my life on the surface, pushing all of my sadness, guilt, fear, and anxiety down so I could survive and make sure those I loved and cared for were taken care of and felt loved. In doing this, I now realize I purposely took care of everyone else so I could avoid dealing with my own shit. In the process, I developed a distorted view of not loving myself or putting myself first before anyone else. Subsequently, I depleted myself and my body shut down. It was no surprise that the shitstorm of 2021 would result in my loss of vision. I was being called to see myself and respond to her—and my entire life—in a whole new way.

***

At this point, I was digging deeper into what else I needed to pull out of my subconscious so I could encourage the light inside me to glow brighter. Over the following months, I ended up doing a deep dive into the woo-woo with readings from various mediums and psychics. Again, I was looking for consistency in their messages to me from the spirit world. Let's just say I definitely got a consistent message and was grateful for the guidance I was receiving from my guides and angels. There was no doubt I was in the midst of something huge that would change my life forever. Life was spinning me inside a cocoon and would not let me emerge as a beautiful new butterfly until I was fully prepared to fly.

By early spring 2022, I was ready for a fresh start. I wanted to be more hopeful and figure out, once and for all, what the hell was wrong with my eyes. Everything with my visual impairment was still fairly fresh and I did not share my metaphysical pursuits with many people who knew me, for fear that I would be judged and deterred from this spiritual path that felt instinctively promising and hopeful to me. I figured they didn't need to know, right? Going out in public was still a big deal because it got old explaining why I had to look over people's right shoulder to see them at all. For someone who had been prone to socializing, it simply exhausted me.

Just when I thought things were stabilizing, my vision changed again. The "other eyes" were still there, staring at me day and night. I had my occasional meltdown, which Stew witnessed, and he was there to calm me down. I managed to maintain a happy face around friends, but I knew some of them saw right through my act and would call me out. My sister was the best at keeping things real and would make me feel like I was normal. She would usually make fun of me and make me laugh so hard I would almost pee my pants. Man, did I need that, too.

During this time I was also trying to figure out how to continue as an active real estate agent. Ironically, when everything in my life was going to hell in a handbasket regarding my health, I was able to work with clients and other agents in negotiating and closed a few escrows. I didn't want to say it out loud or even acknowledge it, but I was getting the sense that my career as a real estate agent might end, and it was devastating.

I worked at Compass and set up a call with my manager, John, the sweetest, kindest, most experienced, and helpful manager I had ever worked with. I filled him in on what was happening with me and my health and asked what he thought I should do. Become a referral agent or quit altogether? For clarity, this means that my new role would have been to connect home buyers with other licensed real estate agents to help them complete the home-buying process. I knew I could trust him. The culture of the entire Compass office was one of family, so I felt safe and supported no matter what.

John told me, "Why don't we see what happens? Don't go referral yet; there are other agents in our office who will help you if you need it. Let's see what happens with your eyesight and we will help you continue as a real estate agent."

His response startled me. I kept hearing Arnold from the '80s show *Different Strokes* say, "What you talkin' 'bout, Willis?" How the hell was I going to work in real estate if I couldn't drive myself to the homes? Even if I got there, would I look like a drunk college girl stumbling into the house?

I told him, "I guess we will see, pun intended."

Accepting his offer, I continued to work as an active agent for a while. I knew I would not be actively looking for clients unless or until my eyesight improved. After talking with John, I made it to some office meetings and felt the love and support from everyone, who helped me feel "normal" and capable.

The next discussion was with myself. While I had the support of my colleagues, I was still negotiating my availability to the technology and tools I would have to learn in order to keep using my computer, phone, iPad, and every other device I relied on in the digital world. Sitting there, staring into the void, realizing you have to relearn everything with "language assist" is no small task and it took me a while to become fluent. Simple things like checking emails suddenly became monumental. I lost it on more than one occasion and blurted, "This sucks!" with my head in my hands, surrendering to it all.

Eventually, I discovered that Apple has an 800 number I could call to get help navigating my keyboard and/or touchscreen so I didn't end up with thousands of emails that went unread because I couldn't see them. The learning curve was huge. There were days I wanted to hurl my laptop through the window, feeling frustrated at the pace of acquiring these skills. Often, it felt like I needed three hands on the keyboard to do anything. The person on the Apple accessibility line would say, very patiently, "To navigate a page you only have to press control, alt, space bar, shift, and up arrow all at the same time." My fingers started cramping. But I didn't give up.

After a few more support calls, with tears disguised as laughter, I was able to figure out how to listen to my emails so my family could stop reading them to me. It was liberating. I felt like I could actually pull this off, continuing to work and play real estate agent. I needed that part of my life grounded in reality because no matter how great Apple support was with helping me learn how to use assisted technology, nobody was there to tell me what to do about the "eyes" I kept seeing, day and night.

I often wondered if the eyes in my visual field were spirits trying to help me or guide me. No matter how much I willed them to stop showing up, they continued to appear. Sometimes I would have conversations with them, just because. Plus, I thought it was funny that not only did I have a vision issue but I was now talking with my friends in the spirit world and saying to them, "You looking at me?" The Mystery remained but was slowly starting to reveal itself.

One day, I heard from a client I hadn't talked with in over two years. His text read: *I was wondering if you might be able to help me sell my four-plex?* I immediately called and I told him I would be more than happy to help sell his property, but there was just this one thing—I had a bit of a vision issue and would he be okay if I brought in another agent to help me with the transaction?

He said he didn't have any issues with me having a vision problem and he looked forward to meeting my associate, too. My amazing friend and fellow Compass real estate agent, Kori, stepped up without hesitation to help me with the property listing. When we walked into the property, though, it was fairly obvious I definitely wouldn't have been able to do this on my own. I tripped on the step and really did look like a drunk college kid after a hard night of partying. However, we got the listing and had the property sold within forty five days. Once that property was sold, I was resolved that continuing as an active real estate agent wasn't going to work and it would be best for me to just be a referral agent instead. I was resolved and okay with it but it sure wasn't what the Universe had planned for me.

A month after my four-plex listing sold, I got a call from a client I hadn't talked with in eight years. We had met at an open house and kept in touch periodically and here he was asking if I could help him sell his house as he stepped into retirement.

At first, I thought, *Are you fucking kidding me, Universe?* But what I actually said was, "Yes, of course I can. But I have to tell you that I have a little vision issue. Would you still be okay working with me and my associate, Kori, in selling your house for you?" Of course he said yes, and we were able to close escrow on his house so he could retire to Arizona. Apparently, the Universe didn't want me retiring into my rocking chair of being a referral agent just yet.

One afternoon, I got a call from a gal who said, "Hi, Jamie, how are you? It's been about four years since we last spoke. Remember you showed me properties and at the time I wasn't quite ready to pull the trigger? Well, now I am ready and I am wondering if you would be able to help me find a home to buy?"

Again, I couldn't believe I was still getting calls. I told her, "Yes, of course I will help, " then explained my situation and the whole spiel. She agreed and we were able to find her dream home in less than a month and close escrow without any glitches. Looking back on all of this, I wonder if I was meant to continue as an active real estate agent solely for these three clients. I will be eternally grateful to Kori especially because she helped me feel normal again. And feeling normal was my new compass.

However, once that third client's house closed, I let go of my practice and put my arms in the air. I had the nagging sense I was being asked to surrender but not give up. Over the next few months, I would grow a deep and intimate relationship with surrender and would realize more and more it was about my willingness *to allow* all that was presenting itself into my life, the eyes and all, including all the people who showed up to encourage me. While I might have let go of my team at Compass, they and so many others had given me my own compass to hold with their support. They cheered for me, encouraged me not to give up, fed me, loved me, pushed me, consoled me, laughed at me and with me, cried with me, supported me, and looked at me with loving eyes; they became my new compass on this journey.

Eventually, I settled into trusting the direction in which I was being led. The Mystery was not as terrifying when I glimpsed the magic of a much larger part of my life. I found peace in hanging up my active real estate agent cape and got cozy in the referral rocker. Even if I would not be seeing my Compass team as often, I felt their support. At peace, I sensed other callings coming into my life, guiding me to what was next.

CHAPTER 14

GOOGLY EYES AND DINGLY BALLS

ONE OF THE SILVER LININGS of surviving Stanford Hospital was that I shed about fifteen pounds and was back to my ideal weight. I wanted to keep the weight off. I would hop on the scale in the bathroom to remind myself of my slenderness, but the Universe was messing with me when I tried to read the numbers. I couldn't see them anymore. Worse, I had to ask a family member, which ended up being Stew, to read my weight.

What should be private between a person and their scale was now an open book for my whole family. Despite my former role as a fitness instructor and coach adept at steering others away from fixating on body image, I was doing the complete opposite. No way in hell I wanted my family to know about the numbers on my bathroom scale. The complex, personal battle women often face with weight became an issue I fiercely guarded when I lost my sight, determined to keep it beyond public scrutiny. My privacy was slowly being eviscerated by the multitude of daily changes affecting my life.

It never dawned on me how much I could hide in my former life. At the beginning, when my right eye was still good, I was capable of reading my emails and responding in a timely manner. Texting was another luxury I took for granted, especially using cute and nuanced emojis that expressed so much more than my words ever could. I could say something funny and sound witty while getting my point across at the same time using a symbol. It was almost like I could be a different person when I texted people than when I talked with them on the phone. All that would vanish.

When I suddenly found myself learning how to navigate the new assist language, I involuntarily gave up any privacy just so I could communicate with the outside world. I have since learned that voice texting is just as effective as using your fingers to write a message; however, this limits what you can say because everyone around you can hear. Complicating matters, when I receive messages, Siri reads them so loudly that my privacy is breached once again. Once, I sent a funny message to my sister and thought I was adding a few emojis by asking Siri to insert them, except when they appeared on her phone, they read: "fart emoji and poop emoji," which clearly didn't have the same effect. I eventually discovered how to send emojis after expanding my skills with the "assist" language, which took a lot of time, patience—and expletives.

There is a wall that anyone who's ever experienced a disability hits when we are bombarded by constant change and emerging technologies designed to help us. I found myself drowning in details and exhausted by the cognitive load it required to adapt. It was like I was suddenly forced to become fluent in a language I had never spoken, nor heard of, in my entire life, and which the majority of people didn't know existed. If Duolingo could invent "assist language" for people who lost their sight, I would gladly study it. My teacher, however, was no one application, just a daily and cumulative hunt for tools, often buried like Easter eggs inside the most common technologies I had relied on. Everything was the same but extremely different. The irony wasn't lost on me. I would often look up in surrender with tears streaming down my cheeks and one word on my lips: *Fuck.*

What hit me the hardest during this transition was the time it took to acquire all the necessary skills to recover my privacy. It was like the universe put me on a slow-motion treadmill and said, "Hey, buddy, there's a lesson in here somewhere. Enjoy the scenic route!" This forced slowing down, however, came with some good surprises. There were just some things I would have to accept I could never do again. When I surrendered, things suddenly shifted. While I had shed some pounds, I was also shedding other things that had been pinning me in bad places.

I never expected to unshackle myself from the non-stop texting spree, let alone mind-numbing emails, trying to keep up with everybody and their dog. My situation had liberated me from this obligation. It was like a soul cleanse, a freedom dance, and a discovery of my "true self" concert all rolled into one. Who knew I could actually breathe without feeling like I needed to be a digital superhero? No more hiding behind my phone, no more fake emails—just the real, unfiltered me. It felt oddly empowering. I said farewell to endless scrolling on Facebook, Instagram, and the TikTok rabbit hole. I used to be stuck in a trance, watching people live their supposedly perfect lives, but truth be told, I was breaking free from that addictive loop fed by filters and façades. Don't get me wrong: I might venture back into those social realms at some point, but when I do, it won't be to showcase a glossy version of my life. It will be to spread a little love, share some hope, and help others see that their authenticity is their superpower.

In my journey to adapt to my "dis-ability" I ended up enabling myself. In fact, I was becoming super-abled. I was feeling more and more confident, but let's face it, I still didn't want my family to know my weight. Because I couldn't really see myself, it was important to have a reliable way to measure how much my body was changing. Numbers did not lie. I needed my scale to help me know where I was so I could stay within a healthy range of the fifteen pounds I had lost in the hospital. I really wanted to keep off the weight because I was unable to walk by myself, go to the gym alone, or do any kind of exercise I once enjoyed without having someone there to either take me or do it with me. I felt like a burden to everyone and this bothered me every single day. I usually worked out by myself, anyway, so inviting another into this intimate routine was not on the top of my to-do list. This was one of the hardest transitions to make, but I knew sitting around was not the solution.

After talking to Stew about my need to weigh myself in private, he found me a talking scale on Amazon. I couldn't wait for it to arrive and when it did, Stew unboxed it for me like it was a ring from Tiffany's, placed it in my bathroom, and left me alone. I was so relieved to finally face my weight in private, but I didn't realize what it meant to have a *talking* scale.

Disrobed and ready to face the truth, I tiptoed onto the scale, making a point not to let a stitch of clothing add an ounce to the numbers. The glass felt cool beneath my bare feet, a sudden reminder of my vulnerability in this moment of truth. As I waited, a brisk breeze from the open window nudged its way in, sending a shiver down my spine. All of a sudden, a robotic, matter-of-fact female voice declared my weight, as if my bathroom had transformed into an unforgiving high-tech clinic. I swear, I attempted to shush the scale, not once, not twice, but three times, hellbent on keeping those digits to myself. But a scale doesn't yield to shushing, no matter how desperately you try. *Did it just get louder?* I wondered, hearing the weight announcement echo.

Standing there in my birthday suit, I couldn't help but think, *Seriously? Is this for real, Divine Forces?* There I was, stark naked, caught in a standoff with a scale that seemed insistent on declaring my numerical truth. The absurdity of the situation couldn't have been clearer. In that moment, I found myself at the mercy of a scale, in a chilly bathroom, contemplating the cosmic joke of it all.

Stew and I were not aware of the volume control and were severely impulsive when it came to any kind of device. We just wanted to rip open the box and use it. Who reads instructions, anyway? Certainly not me and definitely not then. We were not in touch with the volume control and didn't know it existed so I just stood there, while the moody, lady-voiced scale announced my weight so loudly our neighbors might have heard her as well (which is why, perhaps, they stopped bringing me extra baked goods.) I also heard Stew chuckle down the hall and I let out a frustrated laugh. Privacy was slipping through my hands but I wasn't going to let it go without a formidable fight.

I have to admit, I wish this talking scale offered positive affirmations to make the experience more fun. After hearing Ms. Moody announce my weight in her cold tone, I fantasized about a talking scale that had Chris Hemsworth tell me in his sexy Australian accent, "Looking great, babe!" Imagine multiple celebrity voices discreetly announcing your weight and adding, "You look amazing!" Or, " Now keep kicking fitnesses ass!" Or if you needed motivation, "Get your cute ass off the couch and do something!" It might make hearing your weight a little more tolerable and motivating if you could also be reminded you are worth the work to help yourself.

***

With my weight out in the open to my family, I was facing other humiliations daily like wondering if I had food stuck in my teeth or if my mascara was smudged under my eyes. I was reckoning with the fact that I needed help but did not want to rely on anyone for it. I tried to cling tenaciously to my independence, which, let's face it, was preserving my sanity. Ironically, my life was changing so quickly it was forcing me to rely on others for help. The more I needed help, the more I tried to protect my privacy. I thanked God every day for our bidet. At least I knew my underpants would be clean, even if I could not see to check them. As they say, the shit was real, pun intended.

My coping skills were expanding exponentially. I was starting to practice maintaining focus on people in conversation so that they would feel I was looking at them, tracking their faces and expressions as much as I could. While my vision was weakening, my other senses were becoming more and more acute. My ears were picking up on the inflections in their voices so I would know when to nod, look surprised, or soften my face to show compassion. In fact, this kind of close listening helped me absorb everything they were saying without any distractions. I couldn't look off or around them and pretend I was listening. I actually had to listen so intently, I found myself enjoying conversations so much more because of the presence it demanded.

I was feeling so good about this progress and even a little cocky, until my ophthalmologist made a nonchalant comment at a follow-up appointment.

"Your left eye is drifting to the left and down."

"It is?" I asked, surprised.

"Don't worry," he continued. "No one will really be able to tell. I only see it because I am an ophthalmologist and see this often."

I did not feel encouraged. I felt dismayed and wondered how long my eye had been drifting like this. How many conversations had I had when my eye was dropping, even though I was pretending to track whoever was talking to me? My God. What else did I need to deal with? I felt humiliated and wondered how bad it was and asked him if it was going to get worse.

"We can do surgery," he offered, "if it gets to be an issue. But you will be fine; it really isn't that noticeable."

I wanted to believe him. Not about the surgery, but that it was nothing to worry about and that nobody would notice. But how would I ever know for real? I left his office feeling a bit apprehensive, trying to trust that he wouldn't let me walk around with a drifter in my left eye. I thought, *What more can happen to my eyes?* I did not tell anyone what he told me and was too afraid to get anyone else to validate what he'd said.

Then one day I was talking with Grady, who is a compassionate, loving, kind, and sweet mama's boy. While we were having a conversation, I was trying to track him with my eyes. Grady is an honest kid and paused to say, "You know, Mom, your left eye is a little slower to catch up to your right eye when you look straight ahead."

"NOOO!" I blurted.

Grady stayed quiet while I silently went into victim mode, recounting what I'd been through already with the visual impairment itself, diverticulitis, the fistula and queefing, and reconstructed colon. Now I had a googly eye? Seriously? Grady tried to backtrack and make me feel better, but it was too late. I was spiraling. I kept picturing looking like the eyes on the sleep masks that Ellen DeGeneres would have her guest or audience members wear when they were playing a game where they had to be blindfolded. But rather than go down the googly-eye rabbit hole, I made the conscious decision to stop imagining myself like this, and with the support of friends, have been able to keep the dangler in check.

The situation was forcing me to rise above the things that would once make me cringe and feel self-conscious. I began to develop more of my senses, especially with touch, to help when I shaved my legs and other places. Even when I had full vision, this task resulted in some nicks when the razor slipped from my hands in the shower. I had to slow down and really feel what I was doing, especially when shaving my bikini area, which to be safe, I outsourced to the professionals, thank you very much. I was becoming proficient in shaving my legs with minimal razor knicks. With this skill well underway, I could still wear a bathing suit and sunbathe on a pool deck, thanks to my aesthetician, Brittney. She made me laugh when she told me most people don't take care of their backside, which was code for dingly

151

balls. I panicked. *Holy shit* I thought, *what if she finds some on me?* I could not have googly eyes *and* dingly balls.

Thankfully, Brittney assured me I did not have them. I felt relieved and grateful for my bidet. Later, I would laugh at the enormous effort that went into maintaining my dignity in these early days. I would have never shared these conversations with anyone if my eyesight had not been impaired. It put into perspective how much I needed to rely on all of my senses and let the professionals swoop in when the task was beyond my capacity. Dingly balls and googly eyes were not child's play and nothing to mess with—or ever ignore.

I was adapting my senses almost daily to learn to navigate the world blind. It was humbling, humiliating, and even humorous at times. Who knew our eyes were the unsung heroes in the mundane tasks like ensuring a clean behind? As my eyesight took an unexpected vacation, I tapped into my superhero Spidey senses. Listening to others was no longer just a casual, passive activity; it had become a full-on engagement. No more half-listening while mentally planning dinner or plotting my next *Outlander* binge. My eyes were forcing me to be in the here and now with others and with myself. For the first time, I was becoming a super-focused listener from the inside out, and this is how my spirit was making itself heard. I had made space for her. I had stopped talking long enough to let her speak. All I had to do now was listen closely to what she had to say.

CHAPTER 15

PUPPY LOVE

IF THE TALKING SCALE and googly eyes weren't adding to my anxiety—and a growing sense of dark humor—adding a puppy to the household at the same time moved it to the next level. When I first lost my vision, my family had the great idea of getting a puppy. Without asking me, either. If you just heard the record scratch, you were like me: bewildered and feeling a bit brow beaten.

It was a definite WTF moment.

What could have possibly compelled my family to make this decision?

It was their collective instinctual response to an untenable situation.

Mom's going blind! Oh, shit! We'd better get a dog!

Coping mechanisms were in full swing for all of us. But first, let's get one thing straight: I love dogs. I just didn't love the thought of getting a puppy when one, we already had a dog. And two, I was losing my eyesight.

I'm sure if this was a scripted skit on SNL, it would have been freaking hilarious. Why had my family responded this way? When I was first diagnosed, nobody in my family talked about it directly. I was reeling about my situation and trying to talk myself off the ledge with all of the different life scenarios that would possibly be my "new life without vision." At that point, none of those scenarios looked promising nor did they include a puppy as a consolation prize. Instead, I felt hopeless, but I was not going to let my family or friends or anyone I met know this. All my life I was determined never to be a Debbie Downer. But a puppy?

I wanted to look on the bright side. Literally. At this point in my saga, I still had vision in my right eye. Okay. So things weren't that bad, right? Only the left eye was impaired. I had a far-away hope that I would still have the use of my right eye and that only my left eye would be affected by this fucked-up karmic junction. Nobody and nothing, not even a puppy, was going to take away my perfunctory optimistic outlook.

While I was finishing up the antibiotics for my second flare-up of diverticulitis—oh, and also trying not to lose my shit every two seconds—I kept moving forward, as I do, and went about my day helping everyone else and making sure everyone around me was taken care of and heard. At the same time I was going through the motions of my life as my husband and daughter were returning from their trek home from Denver.

I remember standing in front of the bathroom mirror, seeing just my form with my one good eye, feeling like Annette Benning's character in *American Beauty*. She, like me, was a realtor. She had her shit together. She was focused, determined to get the sale. In my case, if I kept a stiff upper lip, kept smiling my way through this situation, I would sell my family and everyone else in my life on the lie that everything was fine. The kids were okay. Stew, too.

"We got this," I'd tell them and flick back my hand in the air. Then laugh so whoever was standing there or listening to me would think, "Well, shit, nothing stops that woman. She'll just keep going and knock down any walls and laugh while she does."

It's hard not to chuckle as I recall this old part of myself. But she was directing the show then, terrified of accepting the reality of the situation. I was going blind. What I was fully aware of was that I would not be sharing the full disclosure with my family. They had to inhabit the house we called our home and there was no way I would allow them to feel threatened by me, my deteriorating vision, and my rapidly changing body.

I had a playbook. My entire childhood taught me one great lesson: how to rely on myself. I was a fighter. A survivor. As the child of a single mother, I had learned all the tricks to keep myself safe, even if they were actually dangerous in the end. They say kids are resilient. They are, until they're not. There is only so much a child can absorb and navigate until their subconscious takes over and they are not aware of the coping mechanisms they've adopted in order to survive the betrayals, disappointments, and inevitable traumas of their life. When that old agreement is still driving the show, as it was when I was diagnosed, the consequences are not kind. I had no boundaries in place to request that everyone help *me* versus me helping them.

When my husband and daughter were arriving in Carmel, they met up with our two sons for lunch. Apparently, they were craving sushi and sitting outside at a restaurant when one of their friends walked by with her new twelve-week-old puppy.

Do I need to tell the rest of the story? It always seems to end—and begin—with that five-letter word. For reasons God only knows, my husband and kids inquired about the sweet puppy. They learned she was a rescue, of course, and there was one puppy left for adoption. In between these sentences, there were obvious squeals of delight, giddy outbursts of joy, and the greatest hope of all—a puppy to save them from the fear of the unknown beast lurking at home they had not fully met and did not want to know: the person I was becoming.

Everyone was on board instantly. Unbeknownst to me, my husband called the puppy rescue organization and told the woman who answered the phone he wanted the puppy. Not one of my family members thought to call me and ask if I would be okay with another dog in the house. We already had our sweet pup, Rocky, who was also a rescue. Considering my situation, why wouldn't my family ask me first? Did they know I would say no? Was I too controlling and instead of asking for permission they were going to beg for forgiveness?

Needless to say, I felt a little bamboozled when they returned home after having lunch with shit-eating grins on their faces. I was so happy to see my daughter and husband, especially after the harrowing week they were gone and I had my second flare-up of diverticulitis. My body was also still recovering from my three-day stint as a "roid junkie," and oh yeah, let's remember I was also losing my vision.

My family persisted and really wanted me to see the puppy at the rescue. I looked them all in the eyes with my one good eye and flat out said, "Uh, no! Hello?! Don't you see what is happening here to me? Probably not the best time to add a puppy to the mix!"

I swear it was like I was in my own bubble screaming at the top of my lungs but none of them heard me. They persisted, and I finally broke down and said I would go with them to see the puppy. Because I could still see clearly out of my right eye, I drove myself there and met the rest of my family at the puppy's foster home. He was a mix between a purebred black labrador and a purebred Australian shepherd. I will admit he was super cute, but I was adamant we were not going to get another dog, especially not a twelve-week-old puppy. After meeting the puppy and satisfying my family's need to torture me, we were getting ready to leave when the woman from the rescue organization picked up the puppy and, with a big grin on her face, said, "Here's your new puppy."

The look on my face was searing. I was so angry and felt so betrayed. We left the puppy's foster home and had a new member of our family tagging along with us. Not one of my family members rode home with me; I was seething and they all knew it.

As kids and husbands do at times, they promised to walk, feed, and train the puppy so he wouldn't be a problem. Rocky was happy to have a playmate and all was good in everyone's world. Little did I know this pup, who we named Koda, would be a blessing not only for my family but for me as well. Rocky must have known with his super-sweet dog senses that his job was done at the age of four years old, because only a short four months after Koda's arrival, Rocky was diagnosed with juvenile lymphoma and passed over the Rainbow Bridge.

Rocky taught Koda everything he could about our family and how we work. He taught him where to go to the bathroom outside and in what area. He oriented him to where he could go in the house. There was a hierarchy he was instilling in the young pup. Rocky got the bed; Koda got the crate. Of course, years later, he found himself in the bed and not just on Stew's side. He only ever naps on my side, leaving his fur all over my organic silk sheets and the lingering scent of his Frito feet. There was an upside, too. Rocky had a menacing bark but it turns out Koda hardly ever barked—only when he was hungry or had to go pee. Having a less vocal dog wasn't bad—in fact, I asked Stew to put different bells on the dogs so I could distinguish which dog was in front of me. Koda's Australian shepherd side makes a shitty guide dog, because he walks in front of me to herd me to where he wants me to go. He's attempted to herd me numerous times and tried to get me to throw the ball he's put in front of me even though I can't see it. This is the game we have been playing now for three years.

Rocky also brought out the labrador retriever in Koda and taught him how to swim in our pool, which made it ideal for getting out zany puppy energy. At first, Koda was afraid of the water, but over time, Rocky coaxed him into the pool and made a game of this, too, until he wanted to fetch the ball. It was as if Koda had a split personality. He wanted to serve, and he wanted to herd, but he could not do both at the same time. And this made him all the more lovable because he was working two jobs day and night when he joined our family.

As a herder, he is the opposite of a guide dog. His agenda, not mine, is usually first. However, there was a time when I was left alone for the first time when Stew left the house to get some coffee. I remember feeling terrified of being alone and tripping on something or falling on my face. To keep myself safe, I sat on our coffee table in the middle of the living room as if it was my safe island, waiting for everyone to return, when Koda came up to me and refused to leave me alone. In that instance, I knew he had come to help me. To this day, when no one is here, he insists on being with me, unless Stew is home because, let's face it, Stew can see the ball Koda puts in front of him.

Over time, Koda developed a distinguished personality. He's a combination of goofy and aloof, and he is an angel in fur. I did not grow up with a dog, but I felt he was like Bodie, the first dog I ever had as an adult when I had two young children. He was a yellow lab and adored all of us. Though I didn't know how to take care of a dog at that time with two toddlers under the age of four, I fell in love with him and felt so lucky to have a puppy nanny who was so good with my kids. Like Bodie, Koda's sweet disposition and gentle ways felt familiar, and I often wondered if it was Bodie who had come back to visit us.

I know I obviously cannot speak for my dog, but I can only imagine he knew Koda was meant to be here with us to be my companion during this time for me to really heal, both physically and emotionally. I truly believe our pets are angels in disguise as they give us unconditional love, are there to make us laugh, are there when we are sad, and protect us when they sense we need it.

CHAPTER 16

A REASON, A SEASON, AND A LIFETIME

HELP CONTINUED TO SHOW UP in ironic ways, not just through a no-service herding retriever.

I love what Walter Winchell said about the true test of a friendship, "True friends walk in when the rest of the world walks out." It seemed like every condition of my life was testing his theory. One of the things you don't see coming when trauma makes a shitstorm of your life is the simultaneous phenomena of the kindness of strangers and revelation of cowards. It was not something I wished to learn. It just happened, like a blister after being burned.

Being a kid who always wanted to find a way to fit in due to moving around so much and the instability of my childhood, I learned to beam a smile, make people laugh ,and be the upbeat person in the room. As a result, I've always made friends easily. All was good. I loved them. And I didn't lose them. But as time went on after I began to lose my eyesight, I began to experience a daunting truth about the stability of friendships. As the saying goes, people come into our lives for a reason, a season, and a lifetime. It's something I've tried explaining to my children, but they roll their eyes because while they hear my words, they can't imagine that the person they call their best friend now might have nothing to do with them a decade or more from now. I tried to explain to them, and again to myself, that people change. Things happen. People respond differently than we might expect. And this might surprise and dismay us. It also might inspire and uplift us. We don't know. It's a play-by-play kind of lesson and you don't learn it until the shitstorms come.

In reality, everyone drifts apart in some way shape or form and heads down their own paths of destiny and if we're lucky, meets up every few years to reminisce about the good old days. But we all generally will drift apart and head in different directions after graduation, maybe connecting a year or two later for a wedding or baby shower. Then, once the family comes and kids are in school or playgroups, a new set of friends is part of your daily life. If you are lucky these friends are with you through the early childhood years to the high school graduation of your children. I heard a saying, *Your vibe attracts your tribe*. This is so true in so many ways. Before my vision got jacked up, I felt like I was doing well navigating all of my friend groups. Looking back now, I want to slap myself in the face for not taking more time to cultivate certain friendships and see the dysfunction in others. But no, I had to have a major medical shitstorm happen to knock me down on my ass, making me look at how I was living my life and who was in it. Were they making me better or did I feel like every time I was around them the life was being sucked out of me? It is an interesting experiment, to see who shows up and stays and who doesn't. I was pleasantly surprised by my friends who stepped up and were by my side from day one, and on the other side of the coin, I was not surprised by those friends who weren't able to be on this ride with me. I don't blame anyone who chose not to stay connected. Heck, some of them I was glad to see go on their merry way, solely because they were energy vampires. But as for the other friends who I miss, I totally understand why they are more distant than expected. This shit is scary and real. Maybe it's that they don't know what to say. A major medical situation, whether it's being diagnosed with cancer, a disability that makes you immobile, or ending up with something like pooping out of your vagina and losing the ability to see clearly through your eyes, can be hard for certain friends for whatever reason. It's the friends for a lifetime I feel have shown up for me these last three years, and I am forever grateful.

As I mentioned earlier, I have a group of college girlfriends who knew twenty-two-year-old Jamie best—we had a damn good time together. I will forever be friends with these women, and even though the years fly by, and maybe we haven't spoken on the phone or seen each other in ten years, once we reconnect, it's like no time has passed and we pick up right where we left off. That is a friendship I will nurture and love until my last day. To be completely honest, I didn't expect any of my friends, old or new, to take such a big role in my recovery. I wasn't really sure what to think when my close girlfriends, who live in my community and who I have known since our kids were little, stepped up and took on the role of not only comforting me but also being there for my husband and children. What a beautiful blessing to know there are selfless people out there who have their own family to deal with who will still take the time to make dinner for you and your family. Who will drive you to your appointment at Stanford to get a drug infusion for two hours and take you to lunch after and drive you back home. Who will sacrifice a whole day to take you up to Stanford Eye Center so you can have the doctors run you through tests for four to six hours and then drive you home, only to have to make sure their family is fed and taken care of, too. Who will pick you up for coffee or lunch dates. Who are kind and nervous about helping you in and out of their cars, getting you set up at a table, and reading you the menu or cutting your food because you look like a cavewoman trying to cut your own food. Who will take you on a walk along a trail you used to go on with them so many times before, but this time you have to tether to them like a two-year-old with a baby backpack and leash so you don't trip and fall on your ass and take them down with you (that might have happened a few times, just to be honest). Who will come over to sit on the backyard patio with you and shoot the shit or who will come over to teach you yoga so you can get your body moving and feel the zen you so desperately want and need.

I believe we are tethered to each other throughout our lifetimes; some of our connections are stronger and last longer than others. I was listening to the book *Sacred Contracts* by Caroline Myss and she says something to the effect of, we have sacred contracts with those who are in our lives. We make these contracts with each other before we are even born. Basically, I signed up for this, and all of those who have stepped up agreed to do so when we were just souls in heaven waiting to be born. It's pretty beautiful and amazing if you really think about it.

But to be honest, I wanted a new contract.

To get one, I had to read over the one in place because I had agreements I needed to update with myself and the Universe if I wanted to heal completely.

***

The Universe has an odd sense of humor about healing.

One morning while I was deep in my despair, wondering why all this was happening, a song popped into my head: "God Only Knows" by the band For King and Country, a Christian rock band. This is not a genre of music I typically listened to but I found myself listening to it at 3:30 in the morning while Koda was sleeping at the foot of our bed in a crate. I don't know if the jingle of his tags on his collar or the words woke me up, but I lay there staring at the ceiling, hearing the lyrics articulate exactly how I felt. That nobody saw me. Nobody would believe what I saw.

I lay in bed digesting these words, still feeling the remorse of my situation. I wanted to ask God, "Why for the love of all that is good in this world did this happen to me?" It was a question I found myself asking all the time and getting mad at myself for doing so. I knew I should not feel sorry for myself. I hated Debbie Downers. I refused to be her. I told myself there were far worse problems in the world. Others were suffering their own losses. I was in a loop of wondering why but slowly realizing I needed to change my mindset so I didn't live the same way as before this happened—and even more tragically, miss the message.

Because meditation and staying grounded had become my focus over the months, I was able to get out of this loop and ask myself helpful questions. How can I heal myself?

What do I need to work on within myself? And because the old me spoke, I had to ask, How do I do this with the inability, at the time, to just Google my questions?

The Universe might have responded to humor because shortly after I began to ask those questions, some conversations were being set in place with old and new friends. These synchronicities led me to specific books and podcasts that would teach me about the power of meditation, grounding, visualization, and energy healing. I devoured these topics and was reminded that spirituality was not new to me.

When I was in my twenties, I had tried valiantly, and sometimes without regard for myself or others, to live my best life. I simultaneously explored the metaphysical world and fell in love with it and all it had to offer. But I only absorbed a small amount of it because everything I did in life at that time was only on the surface. I didn't let anything go too deep into my psyche or spirit merely because I didn't know how to deal with the energy it would have afforded me. Thirty years later, I was being forced to dig deep within myself in order to receive this beautiful light. But what did that look like?

Between the puppy and talking scale, I was starting to navigate my new normal by receiving a little help from the Universe. Companionship and tools were being offered to me and I knew it was up to me to use them. But it took some time. I would stumble and stub my toe—in the proverbial sense—but I would do it alone and without anyone else bearing witness to just how many challenges I was actually facing every single day.

Fear, anxiety, and being FAF (Fake As Fuck) were driving so many of my behaviors, the most offensive being rejecting the help that showed up. Being a self-sufficient person most of my life, asking for help was never easy. It still isn't. I would be lying if I did not tell you it might always irritate me. I would rather give help than receive it. I don't think I'm alone. How many other people felt like me? I would prefer to be in the power position of giving versus the vulnerable position of receiving. Why? Receiving triggered a part of myself I had *literally* turned a blind eye to: being worthy.

Talk about irony. My disability was there to help me see my capability.

If someone had whispered this was the punchline at the time of my diagnosis, I actually might have punched them in the face. Not funny, Universe. Not a joke.

But I could not see any of that then. Rather than focus on what I was gaining, I was mired in the downward spiral of what I had lost and what I was still losing. In the early days of this life-changing experience, my left eye was dark. I saw nothing. Technically, I was blind in one eye. But the right eye still had promise. I could still see light. I could still see the world through "the veil" and so I saw everyone as if through a snowstorm. It was better than the nothing of darkness.

Here's what was happening in the in-between moments after April 2021 when everything came undone: I was being initiated into another way of being in the world. And it scared the shit out of me. I was holding onto the past with a death grip, refusing to let any of it go too quickly or at all. I insisted that my full vision be returned.

Day after day, I prayed to "go back," refusing to see what was happening all around me and, even more so, why. There was a message, but I was too busy listening to the smaller voice in my head that convinced me my eyesight would fully return. I would learn later that when we receive messages involving our eyes, they are usually indicative of not wanting to see something. As a result of our resistance, we turn a blind eye at the very moment when we need to look within ourselves to either connect or reconnect with our spirit and soul. But good Lord. It's so difficult to look at ourselves without seeing what we don't want to see. Here's the kicker. If I had my prior vision and looked into my eyes in the mirror before that day in April 2021, I would have only looked at the surface Jamie, the Jamie I was a master at allowing everyone else to see, instead of the real Jamie who wanted me to see her for the first time.

What I refused to see was a person who was worthy of receiving all the support that was showing up for me: from my husband, my children, my family and friends, to the unexpected "visitors" in my life who offered unconditional love in the midst of my transition. They saw straight through the old Jamie and only interacted with the actual Jamie—a vulnerable yet strong, funny, lovable, capable me who was stronger than I could have ever imagined. The only person not seeing her was me, because I did not feel worthy of her and her power to attract so much goodness, help, and humanity when I needed it most. I failed to see I was not only resourceful, I was becoming a resource for others who felt lost in their own transitions. But why was it so damn hard to see my true self that the Universe felt it particularly poignant to impair my vision?

All my life I'd carried a sense of not being enough and consequently compensated by developing a cheery, optimistic personality that lifted up everyone else around me. The challenge I faced in the midst of losing my eyesight was that part of myself didn't show up for me. Literally. I could not see that part of myself and did not even think to offer it to the terrified little girl still trapped inside me when all of this began.

Although I had not done anything wrong in the biblical sense to inflict this dis-ease on myself, the idea of relying on anyone else to support me did not feel safe. When they did, I was grateful, yet reminded once again that I needed others. This dependence deeply disturbed me. I wanted to drive. I wanted to walk. I wanted to shop. Alone. By myself. But these things were becoming distant activities that were no longer voluntary but logged in my memory of aspects of my life that had died. This left me feeling bereft most of the time. While I passed my perfunctory smile to the world, I felt dejected and disheartened by all of this. Most days it felt overwhelming. On rare days did I see the opportunity it offered—to see aspects of myself that I had buried or forgotten.

The key to all of this, I would come to learn, was being able to be present. First to myself. Then to others. Until I could do that, nothing and no one could help me. I had to show up for myself first. I wish I could say that was easy. The truth is, it was so damn hard. I was not seeing how worthy I was of who I knew I could be, not only as a young girl but as a young woman and now a middle-aged woman rediscovering herself. So what had I done to create this shitstorm? I'd forced my body to shut down and had obscured all of the bullshit I was putting in front of me.

I finally realized all this during a holotropic breathwork class one day. The instructor wanted us to breathe in and out of our mouths while doing what felt like stomach crunches so that we could focus on generating 80 percent of our breath from our bellies and 20 percent from our lungs. I had heard from others that even just fifteen minutes of breathwork could produce a noticeable shift in energy—specifically by activating the life-force energy of well-being. Many people spoke of feeling "high" without any kind of drug. I wanted to know what that felt like. My experience was a bit different, however, and I wondered if the other nineteen people participating felt the same thing: the feeling of an intense overall mind/body/spirit orgasm. It was comical and liberating at the same time and didn't require me to lick any frog poison or take a psychedelic. My body and breath were the only drugs I needed to release my feelings of unworthiness and fear.

At one point I was laughing hysterically, making it hard to maintain my holotropic breathing. I felt so free to laugh so hard and cried at the same time. Something was releasing inside of me, and it felt good. At the end of the session, the instructor told us to do a "CO_2 dump," where we screamed at the top of our lungs. It felt so good to be able to release even more of the sludge that had been sitting in my body and mind for so many years. At the end of the class, she led us through a guided meditation where we visualized our younger selves lined up in front of us. We were to speak kind words to each age of our younger selves. It was fascinating and beautiful. It forced me to consider my younger self and how I talked to her and treated her, and what I wanted to share with her now after all that had happened.

I have come to the realization that in order for me to move forward in my life I have to be present first. Especially in the in-between moments of life, I have to remind myself to be in the here and now. Being present, to myself and the moment, was possibly the most powerful position to heal myself. I wanted to be in this state of mind and strive for it on a daily basis. This kind of presence is possible every single day. Up until my diagnosis, I had never lived like this. I was always living in the future or fretting about the past. I was missing the here and now. My eyes wanted me to see it. So the Universe adjusted my perspective and helped me to see without my eyes.

It has been a long journey. There were weeks and months that passed when I looped back into my habit of belittling myself until my friends who only saw the real Jamie reminded me that it was just my fear driving the bus. We would laugh, too, reminded of the bestselling children's book by Mo Willems, *Don't Let the Pigeon Drive the Bus!* I laugh as I write this because how many of us let the pigeon drive our bus? How many of us allow outdated beliefs to define who we are and determine our course?

The Universe has an ironic sense of humor. Here I was being asked to be present, to see without "eyes," and to know my true self for the first time. With my puppy, a talking scale, and a new list of affirmations that would keep the pigeon away, I was reminded, over and over, that it wasn't me driving the bus, either. It was my spirit. In fact, my spirit was the only driver I could permit to take me anywhere now.

Being present with myself would be challenging but not impossible. If I practiced, it would become the most powerful driver in my life. Presence held it all. If only I allowed myself to see it, feel it, and know it so deeply that nothing could throw me off my path. Ironically, I had been "looking" for someone else to save me. All my life, I had been waiting for another to heal me, support me, feed me, love me, and tell me what to do with my life. This lifelong search for answers outside myself led me back to myself.

The key to my healing was me. I had all the answers, if only I would listen and look for them inside myself rather than rely on everyone else to conquer my fears. I finally saw the truth. I was loved and loving, and I was far more capable of attaining my dreams that were ready to bloom into something beautiful. Most importantly, I was finally able to say yes to receiving help, because I now understood it as compassion in action.

CHAPTER 17

A BEAUTIFUL MESS IN SURRENDER

PRESENCE HAD A PARTNER. It wasn't a solo gig after all. By learning how to be in the here and now, I would also be tasked with surrendering—something I'd grappled with all my life. It didn't take losing my central vision to confront this. *Surrender* sounded like a dirty word, and I refused to say it out loud for fear of jinxing myself. So no, I would not play this game with the Universe any time soon. I was not ready to "surrender" to my condition. And so the battle raged.

The dictionary definition sounded a lot like giving up. I was not a quitter. I did not give up easily. I didn't let others quit or give up either. Aren't we taught over and over that winners never give up? Winners never quit. It's the saying of every motivational poster we've ever seen. It's the poster child slogan of almost every champion athlete. While I was no Olympian, I was no more ready to surrender than accept defeat. Screw surrendering! I was no loser and didn't intend to become one now. I knew I could rise to the challenge of almost anything but suddenly found myself unable to accept my current situation.

It was complicated. I often found my inner child wanting to punch the person who casually mentioned, "All you have to do is surrender." I wanted to ask them if they've ever had to surrender with a capital S, as in Surrender-even-when-it-Sucks Surrender?

I did not see myself among those people who possessed a quiet humility yet fierce inner strength in light of their struggles. I still had more work to do. The lessons in my journey were far from over and some had only just begun. Few people are ever asked to let go. We all want control. We want familiarity. We want what we know and we want it now. Not later. Or decades from now. The ego is a determined little fucker, isn't it?

I loathed this part of the journey. Letting go would not be easy. It's not something most humans easily do; however, life does the teaching when we least expect it. If we survive, we might have a good story to tell. Nobody wants to surrender because we don't want to give up or accept less than we feel we deserve.

Complicating matters, I had nobody who could tell me how to surrender. I mean, seriously—how do you do it? I was not alone in facing this question countless times every day. How do I "surrender" to my current situation in order to move forward in my life if I can't even say the word out loud or know what *surrender* actually means to me?

First, nobody told me surrender was a multi-tiered experience. It wasn't like a once-and-done thunderstorm. That would be far too easy to endure and survive. What I found out is that surrender would consist of *at least* three stages, the first of which I would find the hardest to endure. This is the stage of the chrysalis. Of being pinned inside a cocoon but wanting to be free and, conversely, of resisting going into the chrysalis at all and instead remaining the caterpillar.

Denying myself the truth I was actually going blind was my way of resisting the chrysalis. Sue Monk Kidd writes in her touching book, *When the Heart Waits*, about transformation in mid-life—how the caterpillar is often very resistant to undergoing the chrysalis and will do anything to avoid it, not aware of the beautiful transformation waiting to happen.

How many of us can relate? I was like a toddler, kicking and screaming, pleading with the Universe to slow its roll on my vision impairment. I braced myself, every single day, for almost three years, hell-bent on rejecting my actual reality. I was changing but did not want to change. So many parts of my old self were dying, but I was silently kicking and screaming to keep them alive. I clung and clung and clung to my old self for dear life, but deep down, my spirit knew what it had signed up for: big change. But humans don't easily reach out for change. We spend most of our time resisting the very experience that is leading us to our next best chapter. But because I had no idea what that would be, the mystery terrified me and kept me spinning in place. I was forgetting one key universal truth that no human can deny: change is the only constant and the only sure truth across every culture on the planet. Who was I to believe it would exclude me? If anything, the process of being inside the chrysalis was begging me to allow it to envelop me, spinning me inside its silky, sticky web so I could transform into the most beautiful, meaningful expression of myself.

A friend once asked me if I knew the difference between a butterfly and a fly. I had no idea. She explained it to me like this, "The butterfly comes out of the pupa and the fly comes out of the poop-a." I believed her and laughed. It was a simple answer with truth. I could relate to the pupa coming out of the poop-a. Some days it felt like I was truly emerging from shit. But most days I was avoiding looking at it or even owning that this was where I was in the journey—resisting change, just like the classic hero's journey. I was the protagonist in my own story who wanted to forfeit all this change and just get on with the butterfly stage. After all, creeping around the ground took a lot more effort, it seemed, than flying gracefully through the air, above the sludge. In theory, I wanted to fly. In practice, I could not get out of my own resistance to enable the kind of transformation I desperately needed to undergo if I had any hope of thriving. Until then, I was in the survival stage. The chrysalis, via my vision impairment, was the invitation and initiation into my highest potential. Losing my vision felt like a damn high price to pay for that, so I lingered in the lower vibration, where I believed I was safe. In truth, my freedom was being held inside the butterfly I had yet to allow myself to become. This was an inside job and all my spirit guides, angels, and the Universe waited patiently for me to wake up and claim the opportunity.

I no longer wanted to be the caterpillar. And I especially did not want to be a fly. I wanted to transform into a butterfly but falsely believed that once I emerged, my vision would be restored. Day after day, I told myself I would see again, instead of honoring the present moment and truth of the day—I could not see, could not drive myself anywhere, could not shop by myself or walk down the street by myself. The list goes on and it was evident my denial was keeping me from taking these next best steps. I was just too afraid.

Why? Deep down, I knew I was being led into something beautiful. Transforming into the butterfly was something I knew I wanted and needed. In order to do that, I knew I had to be present with myself and stop telling myself stories about where I was or where I was going. There was no destination or arrival in being present, and that blew for me. I desperately wanted the assuredness of such seismic change, yet none was guaranteed. But when I began to really think about how a hearty caterpillar sets itself up to escape the bullshit around it, the idea of transformation started to appeal to me. It can snuggle inside its cocoon, even if the wind blows, because it has a secure attachment. Nothing can shake that sense of connection, and so the hearty caterpillar feels safe to decompose and release all unnecessary baggage. It transforms from deep within its soul to become what it was always meant to be. When the time arrives and the transformation is complete, the once hearty caterpillar breaks free of its now too small and confined cocoon. In my case, it would take divesting myself from years of negative core beliefs and behaviors that no longer served me; however, the results would be significant. Breaking through the veil that held the caterpillar in place for the time it needed to transform yields a new, glorious, colorful being—a butterfly that can spread her wings and fly fearlessly and effortlessly because this is who she was meant to be all along. Free in her new form, she can soar to great heights and enjoy all the sweetness her new life has to offer. I wanted to become a butterfly. I didn't want to go through the torture of the transformation, but I understood the mechanism at work. Every human being on the planet will go through some transformation but it is up to us to choose to do the work and stay in the goo—so that we can grow wings and then fly.

Raising my family near Pacific Grove, I loved taking my kids to the butterfly sanctuary when they were little. We were in awe of the beautiful serenity we witnessed there. The images of those butterflies floating and swirling around me and my children brought back so much joy and reminded me we are a lot lighter and stronger than we think. While I was still shedding my baggage in the pupa/goo, I realized if I could sit with myself in this stage and know I was exactly where I was supposed to be, then the time would come when I could fly in the direction of my true destiny. *A butterfly,* I told myself over and over, *knows how to fly.* The only problem was I still did not know how to surrender. It was not instinctual.

While I tormented myself by wishing I could just "give in" and accept what happened so I could move on with my life, something else was gnawing away at me. Something else wanted to be known. But I clung to my version of "surrender" and thought I just needed to give myself permission to be a cane-tapping, dark-glasses-wearing, touchy-feely, depressed codependent. The truth is that wasn't what my spirit wanted. That wasn't what the Universe had in store for me when it presented me with the decision to surrender. And I had a *long way* to go before I saw it as an opportunity.

I knew my ego would be totally fine with the scenario because accepting that kind of existence seems logical and what most people would think I *should* do. But my soul was saying something else. Every day, she was patiently whispering in my ear to believe in myself, to listen to the answers that showed up in front of me, and to pay close attention to the connections that were being made with those who would help me.

Surrender, as it turns out, was initiating me into being present, which had always been extremely hard for someone like me. Perhaps you're like me in wanting instant gratification. The quick win. The closed deal. I wanted it all and now. But surrender and spirit do a funny dance, especially for people caught up in a trauma loop. I was slowly starting to realize that maybe my vision was connected to past traumas and I needed to "surrender" my need to keep doing, achieving, earning, and feeding my shame in order to stop the trauma loop for good.

Until then, my whole life had been a lesson in survival. It began at birth, when my mom was going to give me up for adoption then slid into the moment I had to get off the school bus alone when I was five years old and use my trusty house key on a string to open our front door while my mom was at work. As a classic latch-key kid of the '70s, I would go into the house and call my mom and let her know I was home. She wouldn't be coming home for another four hours, so I would grab a bowl of cereal and sit in front of the television, watching cartoons and kid shows until she got home.

The roles quickly reversed when I was eight years old and found myself taking care of my very depressed mom when she returned home from work every day. Then two years later, when I was ten, I found myself protecting my sister and myself from predators while we were alone at home.

The feeling of instability continued. When we moved during middle school from Kansas to California, I learned how to adapt to new friends and a new way of life. We struggled to find a home we could afford and had to live with friends and family for at least a year until my mom found permanent housing. The trauma loop intensified in high school when I refused to tell anyone about being sexually assaulted for fear of not being believed and validated, and because of the shame of it all. Without any practices in place to heal, I packed this compounded trauma with me after college when I moved to Hawaii. I had $800 in my pocket but no job or place to live. I was just twenty-four years old with a one-way ticket to finally do something for myself. That plan quickly backfired when I realized I needed to be more responsible and get a job that gave me health insurance, a 401k, and a salary I could live on.

A few years later, with some life experience under my belt and a new lease on life and work in California, my new job as a merchandiser for a wine distributor gave me perks but also peril when my male coworkers sexually harassed and demoralized me. The trauma was well and alive, jabbing me in the gut every so often to nudge my spirit out of the driver's seat. For the next twenty years the trauma festered unchecked while I expanded my universe by getting married, raising my children, and helping my husband pay the mortgage with multiple jobs along the way. Untreated trauma, like a cavity that is never remedied, decays like a tooth and leaves a hole.

Eventually, the foundation I had built on the sands of my trauma came crashing down during the pandemic, as I imagine it did for many others who were not prepared to "surrender" to what was happening. A year after lockdown, I underwent major abdominal surgery to have a shorter colon and to stitch up a hole in my bowel so I didn't poop out of the wrong hole. Nothing like dark humor in the midst of a global pandemic. This was followed by an appendectomy then the removal of my gallbladder, all on top of losing my eyesight in the span of one year. Call me crazy, but surrendering did not appear to be an option. If anything, I clung tenaciously to everything else so that I could avoid facing my reality or doing anything to heal my trauma.

What was happening? Why was it happening? How could I stop it?

The Universe was throwing curve balls at me and watching how I responded.

I could not accept that I might have played a role in creating this situation.

That was the kind of Surrender that Sucks. I wasn't there yet.

I did, however, wonder about the concept and possibility of soul contracts—what spiritual practitioners have for millenia described as our way of creating the events in our lives in order to learn what we needed to learn to evolve in this lifetime. If that was true, it goes without saying that humans are wired to be Olympic-level survivors. Even so, asking anyone to surrender is like the greatest affront to their will and resilience. Who would surrender after going through all that? I was perplexed, angry, and terrified. Was I supposed to just wave the proverbial white flag and smile?

If surrender meant giving up and just giving in to the situation point-blank, I felt betrayed by all that I had gone through. Let's be honest: I believed and expected some kind of small mercy, a reprieve, or maybe a few more magic mushrooms.

But the funny thing is I came to realize surrender meant something else.

SHOULD'VE SEEN THAT COMING

One day close to the two-year anniversary of losing my eyesight, my husband and I were in the car discussing the future and how I saw mine. I mentioned the word *surrender* and how I was struggling with the word and its meaning. He asked me what it meant to me. I told him right away it was giving up or accepting. Hearing those words come out of my mouth made me sick to my stomach. I refused to give up or accept any of what had happened to me. He gave me a look, which I could sense said, *You need to check yourself before you wreck yourself, babe.* I could hear his voice crack. Stew rarely if ever displayed emotion and we had used humor to diffuse it most of our marriage. To hear the quiver in his voice gave me pause. He was truly concerned about me. To him, I had just given up—not only the fight but any hope of getting better.

What was happening in those god-awful weeks inside the chrysalis was the spinning of a message out of the threads of my trauma, begging me to listen. Here's what I heard: *you can heal yourself.* Excuse me? The message was persistent. *You can heal yourself.* Even though I heard the words, I did not grok the meaning. How do I heal myself when I can't even surrender to what has actually happened to me? Couldn't the Universe see I had done everything under the sun to help myself not lose my eyesight? I'd sought the finest doctors at Stanford. They had no insights into why this all happened. The only thing we agreed on was I had systemic inflammation throughout my whole body, the vessels in my eyes were the weakest point, and the COVID-19 vaccine was the last straw to break and issue me the "diagnosis" (nudge nudge, wink wink) of optic neuropathy.

I sought the expertise of doctors at the Mayo Clinic and UCLA Medical Center, both of whom said they couldn't help me either and that Stanford did everything they would have done. Even with all of that, I should have been able to finally wave my white flag of surrender, but my ego wasn't having any of it. I explored the Eastern medicine path with energy healing, mystics, and mediums, hoping they would be able to help me get my eyesight back to normal. Every morning I would wake up with the veil covering my sight and not having the ability to drive myself or have the independence I once took for granted, I would yell in my head, *WHY!? WHY THE FUCK IS THIS HAPPENING TO ME!!? WHAT DID I DO TO DESERVE THIS!?* I was so damn sad. How the hell do I heal myself when all I have in my head are pity parties?

I attempted to hide this less-than-helpful mantra from my family and friends. I used humor and deflection to make sure those who loved me and even those who I'd just met were all okay with my vision impairment. But I got in my own way. I did not want their pity or help because that would mean I had "surrendered," and I refused to feel the seering shame of that.

All these emotions strummed in and out of my body and spun me in all different directions emotionally. As time went by, first one year, then the second, and now the third, I chose to take a breath and reflect on why I was doing this to myself and what surrender meant to me. Why was I fighting it and how could I heal myself?

I found myself sitting quietly outside the house one day when everyone was gone. For the first time I was able to sit and let my spirit talk to me about how to handle this situation and how to move forward.

She had been trying to talk with me even before all of this went down in April 2021, but of course I did not listen. She yelled at me, whispered to me, gave me stomach aches and signs and symptoms but I still ignored her. Now, I was ready. Tired of fighting and swimming upstream against the currents of doubt, sadness, and fear, I finally listened to her this time. She said to be still, to listen to my breath, to know that everything was going to be okay. She whispered that I need to have the willingness to go with what comes next. She said I can heal myself and I know how to do it. I have to just believe in myself. She said the most important piece of healing is to be present. After this reflective time with my spirit and after some deep dives and discussions with friends and family, I took the time to finally reconcile with this beautiful mess in surrender. It might always be messy. And that would be okay.

For the first time in a long time, I started to make healthier choices. I did yin yoga, not only because each pose was held for five minutes and that meant I wouldn't fall on my face doing the asanas. I also did some half-ass meditation when I was by myself at home but I was able to really get into a deep meditation when I went to a sound bath or sound healing. I started seeing a naturopath and subsequently began taking supplements. I also changed my diet and took out inflammatory foods, which pretty much meant eliminating most of the foods that brought me joy. I started grounding myself and sitting outside in nature daily. I was learning how to be still and how to expand my community with like-minded people.

Most importantly, I made a promise to myself. I was beginning to listen to my spirit more carefully and reminded myself I was worth this amazingly beautiful wave that I was riding. I reminded myself of how many people had come into my life to lift me, love me, and remind me of my strength and fortitude and courage to surrender. Even if I hadn't done so yet, I was trying.

***

Two songs looped in my head during this battle: "Let it Be" by The Beatles and "Let it Go" by Idina Menzel from the movie *Frozen*. Both songs carried an important message, which I chose to ignore because who wanted to let anything go or let anything be? Not me. Not then. I wanted to hold it all—my sadness, grudges, fears, insecurities—and permit them instead of my spirit to define me. I stubbornly kept everything locked deep in the bowels of my gut, which is part of the reason it was so messed up. It all made sense.

So how does anyone let anything go? It felt easier said than done.

I was really good at telling myself I was not going to worry about what happened and move forward. Nice try, right? I was clearly avoiding all the emotional baggage I was still lugging around with me. I sought therapy to unearth what was keeping me down and underwent EMDR to help with trauma but continued to struggle.

Surrender was not coming easy or fast. I grappled with the contradiction inherent in surrendering in order to manifest what I wanted to happen. How does that work? If I was being asked to surrender to what my life was, how could I manifest what I wanted? I was so confused.

It's not like I was totally off the rails. I had made it a daily habit to ground myself and sit with my thoughts of what I wanted my life to look like. I was doing all the things that the book, *The Secret,* by Rhonda Byrne, said to do and following all the self-help books. I knew what I wanted. That was easy. I wanted to see! I also knew what I didn't want: this veil in my face 24/7. I wanted to drive myself to the store and really anywhere the hell I wanted to go. I wanted my optic nerves to heal and be the beautiful salmon-pink color they were supposed to be, not the pale-pink pallor color they had become. I wanted to see my face in the mirror and make sure my makeup did not make me look like a clown or Phyllis Diller, as my mom once relayed after I put some blush on one day. I wanted to go for a run, and I hated running. I wanted to take my dog on a walk without having to take someone else with me. I wanted to cook dinner—or any meal for that matter—for my family and friends. I wanted to walk aimlessly through Target and Home Goods just because I could and buy stupid shit I probably didn't need but would convince myself I did. I wanted to pick my friends up and take them to lunch instead of having them always pick me up. I wanted to drive my youngest child to school before he got his license and not miss that special time to talk about all that was going on in his life. I wanted all of this.

This pity party exhausted me. It was draining the life out of me. I had to learn that life is what it is. We are souls having a human experience. We have free will and can choose how this human experience plays out. That's the beauty of life. My body had held on to so much good, bad, and ugly for more than fifty years. Of course it would take me a minute to work through everything. I had to remind myself this was a process. If the outcome I wanted in my life was to become a reality, then I had to do the work.

What did that mean? I had to be willing to let go of all of the hurt, fear, shitty moments, sadness, and everything else that had been festering inside my body so I could clear space for the beauty, love, and abundance I sensed was possible in my life. Because I now understand: visualization without intention is just a daydream; visualization with intention is reality. I needed to live my reality.

Nearly three years into this mess, I had not been able to admit what I knew to be true. But the gig was up. The message was loud and clear. If I could surrender and let go of the need to control my life, then I could begin the process of manifesting how I would like it to unfold. I did not need my eyesight to forge ahead with that. All I needed was to walk off the merry-go-round that was making me miserable. I was so focused on what I had lost that I had forgotten to claim what I still had left. I had agency. I had a voice. I had a will. I was not alone, but exactly where I needed to be. In the midst of the mess, I had finally arrived fully whole unto myself. And now, the healing could begin.

CHAPTER 18

MEETING MDMA

WITH THIS ADMISSION, I sensed it was time to dig a little deeper into my psyche. That was a code way of saying I needed some help confronting my demons and decided a little help from "Molly" or MDMA, whose full name—methylenedioxymethamphetamine—I could barely say, was the next best thing to frog poison. Not that I expected too much from taking what the kids used to call ecstasy, but when a trusted friend suggested a safe way to use this empathogen to clean the inner barnacles off my boat, so to speak, I said yes to the opportunity. I felt stuck and was ready to release anything that was willing to free itself of me, including, if I'm honest, my refusal to accept I was going blind. As if the empirical evidence wasn't enough to convince me.

So I went with eyes wide open, aware of the risks and possible rewards of using Molly as medicine to help me. Not only might I feel euphoric and more connected to everyone and myself than I had ever felt in my life, I might possibly experience the severest depression, too. Oh, and mood swings. And dehydration, which was the least of my worries. I convinced myself the benefits far outweighed the risks and elected to undergo this psychic adventure in October 2023.

My understanding about going on an MDMA journey was that the love drug would help me experience no fear. Honestly, I didn't even know this was possible. Was it even possible to have no fear? Was that even human? I figured fear was like gravity. We could not live without it. It was a force that drove every one of us on a constant basis. I could not remember any time in my life when I had not had at least one thing that scared me each day. Didn't everyone have the kind of fears I had? The fear of my kids getting sick. Or run over. Or shot by a lunatic on a killing spree. Or maybe more mildly, the fear of the guy who cuts me off in traffic, then flips me off to punctuate his impetuousness while my heart is racing and my hands are clenched on the steering wheel, feeling as though I had miraculously escaped an accident. Nope. I did not know what it would feel like to live without fear—and I began to wonder if this love drug was akin to a hyperbaric chamber, allowing me to experience life as if I were floating around on the essence of love itself no matter what I was facing or experiencing.

That said, MDMA appeared very appealing. It would be like taking a truth serum but not suffering from any negative emotion as a result of seeing what's true. And, let's face it, most of us run away from what's true because it often hurts—or means we need to change something or let go of something that isn't serving us, like the binky we love but that is going to give us buck teeth if we don't stop using it. All these thoughts swirled around me when I weighed the pros and cons of going on this medicine journey. It would be the last of the bunch—and seemed like a complimentary closer after starting with the shaman of Big

Sur. If he could summon spirits on my behalf, maybe Molly could summon me to myself and wouldn't make me scared to see her, perhaps for the first time, without two eyes but from within. Guess what? I was scared.

I had no idea what to expect. Would the MDMA medicine compel me to strip down to my birthday suit and dance around the house? I was a newbie at this psychedelic world, having never participated in its heyday at raves and parties in the '80s. And much like those parties, this medicinal trip would apparently take six hours, more or less, but was the equivalent to five years of therapy. It seemed like a cost-efficient and time-saving device to dig deep.

So off I went that fateful fall day to a trusted friend who had years of experience guiding people through their psychedelic journey. I came prepared this time, unlike the other experiences I underwent, having done research on MDMA and several other psychedelics like ayahuasca, ketamine, and psilocybin mushrooms. Of all the choices, MDMA was the right medicine for me. It was designed to help people with severe trauma and PTSD, formulated to create the feeling of love, not fear, which made it appealing. Everyone has their own unique needs and must only work with practitioners who honor that. I felt blessed to have an experienced guide.

When I walked into her house and smelled the protective smoke of *palo santo*, I knew the space was full of clear energy. *Palo santo*, apparently, is stronger than sage for clearing negative energy from buildings and from our own aura, the signature, seven-layered energetic field that surrounds our bodies and corresponds to our seven chakras. With the clearing smoke of *palo santo* protecting me, I felt safe to tell my truth to the guide. She invited me to sit down at her kitchen table, asked me a few questions about the journey, then instructed me to pull five angel cards from an oracle deck, which happened to be spot on with all the things my spirit needed me to address. I pulled:

Victory
Teaching and Learning
You Know What to Do
Patience
You Are Safe

She administered the first part of the journey then led me from the kitchen to her living room where I laid on a bed while the medicine worked its way through my body. She played the list from my bespoke MDMA Spotify playlist and helped me feel safe. About forty minutes later, when the medicine kicked in, I felt nauseous as if I was inside a lava lamp. I took some deep breaths to let the medicine flow and soon began to notice things. Thankfully, I kept my clothes on and proceeded to stay in one place for the entire journey, but to my surprise, I began talking non-stop, out loud, as if my body needed to voice what was happening to me.

After my guide administered a second dose about ninety minutes into the journey, I kept talking non-stop, as if I was channeling—for the next *five-and-a-half hours*. My guide had never witnessed anyone do that during an MDMA journey. Apparently I talked for so long that my mouth hurt and felt dry. I asked everything and anything. At one point, I asked God if I could say, "God damn," because I was always told it was blasphemous to say the Lord's name in vain and had always chastised anyone who did. I was surprised by God's glib response, "You're fine. Just don't say it in a mean way." This startled me. I had judged so many others for saying these words but God was telling me it was no big deal. Just be kind about it. The revelations continued. I saw past lives. I talked to Jesus. I saw my children. I saw what their lives would be like and how many children they would have. I had never experienced anything like this. The inner knowing was so powerful, I actually doubted it. Especially this: when I listened to the recording later, I heard myself saying very early on, "I can see. I can see." The entire experience was fascinating, and I am so grateful I recorded the entire six-hour journey on my phone. While it would be painful to relisten and glean these truths, I wanted to share an unedited excerpt that held the key to freeing me from my struggle.

"So scary, all by myself. Sitting there, my eyesight is fading. I don't know what is happening. There is darkness in my eye and no one is caring. No one is asking questions. I am playing it off like it's no big deal but it's fucking scary. What was that dark spot in my eye? Why was it there? I didn't know what to do, I didn't know who to ask. I didn't know who to call. I asked my optometrist and he sent me to an ophthalmologist, who was so cold.

It scared the shit out of me, I was all by myself. I knew I wasn't dying but I knew I was going to lose something precious, and I was so fucking scared. There was no urgency. No one was advocating for me. I had to advocate for myself. I was making decisions based on fear.

My eye filled up, my eye filled up, it's filling up, it's like water, I can see liquid. It's so fucking scary I don't know what to do. No one is listening to me. What's happening, what's happening? Am I going to go blind? What's happening? I know the veil is there, I know the veil is there. I am not going to go blind, I am not blind. I had to have this happen.

This happened because it is part of my journey. I knew it was going to happen. I called it, I called it. I would watch things where people were blind and I would say to myself, 'God, I hope I don't become like that.' That was the Universe saying, 'Hey, bitch, it's going to happen.' You are not going to take care of yourself, you are going to worry about everyone else. You are going to forget that you are loved. You are going to forget all of it.

So we are going to make you remember, we are going to make you shift. We are going to make you breathe. We are going to make you see things you didn't think you could see that you knew all along, that you knew as a two year old, you knew you had people around you, you had spirits around you, you knew as a baby, You knew as a baby, you came to this world and you knew, you knew, but you couldn't see it yet, you couldn't see it yet, you still couldn't see it.

We had to put the darkness in your eye, we had to, you weren't seeing it, you were hiding behind the veil, you were hiding. You were hiding from so many things. Why were you hiding? You are beautiful. You don't need to hide. People love you. People think you are funny. Yeah, you say things that are kind of embarrassing sometimes, but it's funny to you. So much light around you, you are so light. We had to do this, we had to put the darkness in your eye. We had to put it in your body on the left side. We had to, we are not sorry, we are not sorry that we did that. We had to do it. We love you. You asked us to do this, you asked us to do it this way.

We are only following your direction. And we knew you would be scared, you told us you would be scared, you told us you would struggle, you told us you wouldn't want to surrender to it, you told us all of this and we believed you and we knew we had to, we had to fill your eye with darkness, we had to. But your nerves are regenerating, everybody says they aren't but they are. Your optic nerves are regaining their color, that pink, salmon, beautiful color, the oxygenated blood is flowing into your optic nerves. Oh, yes, because, Jamie, you, you can see so many things. You can see so many things. So many beautiful things. You can see them with your eyes. Your eyes will clear, you will see in 3D, you will see your children's faces. They are so beautiful. There is so much to say, there is so much to say! Oh, God!

My mind was so open and I was able to ask my subconscious the questions that only it could answer. It was surreal and so beautiful. One significant message that came from this experience was my body and mind telling me what I already knew but wasn't accepting. It was the big bad word that is *SURRENDER*. This whole time I thought I was surrendering, but I was not doing that at all. I was resisting. I was fighting every thought or action of surrender. The MDMA journey figuratively opened my eyes to what I was not doing, what I needed to do, and how to do it. Three words kept flashing in my mind's eye: *trust, believe, accept*.

Since I had already created this situation, I had the solution, too. It all bubbled up through the MDMA journey: I would need to *trust* in the process I was living through. If I could trust what I was experiencing and be there inside it fully, it would move me in the direction of being present in my life, and that kind of presence would bring me an inner peace I had yet to live.

The second word, *believe*, was there to remind me of all the possibilities of what I could still do, what I had left, versus staying fixated on what I had lost. I had to see what remained. It was like the Universe had rescrambled things for me and gave me the agency to put the pieces back together better. What might have seemed like an end-of-the-world scenario, which made me feel sad, might actually be the portal into living an expansive life beyond my wildest imagination. I needed to believe in the healing light that existed inside me so I could trust how to handle whatever circumstance I faced. Believing in possibilities, it turns out, is one of the five aspects of post-traumatic growth—a little bonus the Universe tossed into the bag.

The third word, *acceptance*, was the hardest word for me to embody. It is no surprise that acceptance is also the final stage in dealing with a death. My old life, way of being, and way of seeing had died. I did not want to accept this. I had done a ton of bargaining with every kind of modality that might magically restore my sight. None of them did. I had been pissed at myself for not taking better care of my health over the years. I had checked anger off the box. I had even been in denial, refusing to say the B-word and laughing at the thought of getting a service dog. But I had finally come to the final ledge on this journey, which represented the deepest chasm I was expected to cross. It was more than terrifying to accept what had happened and, even more so, to accept the present moment with its continued cycle of Mystery and unanswered questions. But the jig was up. Acceptance would actually give me wings to make that leap—and fly.

This was not the path I had ever consciously wanted, but the MDMA journey helped me understand it's the path I chose for myself before I had even taken on a body in human form. It also helped me shed the fear covering my whole body, which felt like slime and held me back from moving forward, seeing the beauty around me, and even reaching out for help. Shedding this made me feel a hundred pounds lighter and come to terms with my truth. I was blind but did not have to be ashamed of this disability. By finally accepting what I had chosen all along, I was able to greet the path I found myself on and fully surrender to it.

The struggle was over. The fight was gone. I was here. Now. Fully embodying all of my truth. Now that the Divine knew I had embraced these three words, I was able to surrender. For some people, the ability to trust, believe, and accept comes instantly. For others like me, it can take years, and sometimes a lifetime, before surrender feels as involuntary as breathing. But I had arrived at the ledge. I took a breath, accepted, trusted, and believed in whatever came next.

CHAPTER 19

GROUNDED FOR LIFE

THE OLD SAYING IN THE healing community, "Give a healing, get a healing," soon resonated deeply with me after I chose to show up for myself completely. After uncovering my deepest fears with MDMA, I was ready to say yes to what came next. The second that I showed up for myself, others began to show up for me. The Universe was introducing me to those who sought what I had come to learn. It was almost as though I was being offered a mirror to see how much I was growing and letting go, and it dawned on me I was becoming a teacher.

The time had come for me to share my experience. The first opportunity offered was to talk to a family friend who had literally been hit by a sledgehammer. You can't make that up. Until then, this saying always seemed metaphoric, but this was the first time I had ever known anyone who had actually been struck by one.

My friend Raul is a firefighter who was working with his crew dismantling a training prop when his rotary saw got stuck. In order to release it, it needed to be tapped with a sledgehammer. Consequently, the sledgehammer ricocheted off the rotary saw that he was holding while he was on a ladder. When the sledgehammer ricocheted off of the saw, it hit Raul in his helmet. The impact caused severe head trauma and rendered him unconscious for a few moments—but long enough to cause some brain injury. After regaining consciousness, Raul could not immediately recognize or remember certain people and events in his life that had played a significant role. Devastated, he continued to experience severe lapses in his memory and was terrified of how his life would look after the Universe literally dealt him this blow.

When my husband and I went over to his house to bring his family dinner and help jog his memory, we were happy to hear him say he remembered us, and subsequently our connection to him and his family. While sitting near him, I waited to make sure and just held space for him. I knew instinctively that what he had gone through was life changing, exhausting, and hard to verbalize. I could feel all of this coming from him. I knew those feelings because I had gone through a similar life course correction barely two years earlier.

During our brief visit that evening, I could sense that Raul wanted to share something with me. Again, instinctively, I asked him specific questions to try and pull out any uncertainty he might have in sharing any strange or synchronistic events. He shared with me a few encounters that both scared him and made him feel pure love and calmness. He was afraid that if he shared any of these encounters with anyone they would think he was crazy. I assured him that he was talking with the right gal, and that I totally understood him. I could sense his body lighten and not feel so burdened; it was so beautiful to witness. Toward the end of our visit, he turned to me and said, "You are so shiny. Every time I look at you there is a bright light all around you; it's so cool." I was speechless and a little embarrassed, too. I loved that he could see my aura.

I stayed in contact with Raul over the following weeks and promised I would always listen to his encounters and truth, if he needed me to know. As he got better and his memories returned, he told me he was disappointed because he wasn't able to see people's auras like he had before. I reminded him he still had that ability, but it was just packed away for a minute so that his body and brain could heal. The insights poured out of me with complete certainty. For the first time in my life, what I knew and what I was saying was coming from a place of sovereignty. I doubted nothing. Instead, I felt at ease and calm, holding space for my friend in his moment of uncertainty. I could trust what I knew. What I said. What I saw for him. And for myself. And for many others who would show up in my life.

I explained that when he was ready to embark on stepping fully into his inner light and spirit then all of those abilities would no doubt resurface. I also shared with him that if he could stay aware of the synchronicities happening all around him, they would help to remind him of those gifts he was given. Then I told him what I had learned myself: his life would be even more beautiful than before the trauma. He didn't need a sledgehammer to wake him up to what was always beautiful, but there it was as a tool for his own becoming.

This truth resonated deeply with Raul and gave him peace. When he told me I looked "shiny" I realized that my role as a teacher was to reflect back to others their radiant self—whole, complete, and perfect. No injury or illness, accident, or any other misfortune could take away anyone's true essence. It was all perfect and all love—and it was somewhat cruelly comedic we made it so hard to see. The irony wasn't lost on me that I'd had to lose my vision in order to see this, too.

Being on this new life path and navigating it without letting my ego and self-doubt take over has been a lesson in itself. I discovered that being present afforded me the magic of synchronicities more often than I had ever experienced. Those synchronicities could be as simple as a phone call from a friend who I happened to just think about who called or texted the same day. Other moments could be as profound as being at the right place at the right time, enabling you to fulfill a lifelong dream, meet the love of your life, or be presented with an opportunity that turns out to be one of the best things that has ever happened. The list goes on. The lesson was to sit in the present and observe what was showing up and why. This was the actual act of surrender, and I realized it was what I was being called to teach.

My only job was to hold space for myself and others. At first, I did not understand this concept, which was introduced to me by a friend. One day, she gently told me, "I will hold space for you." I thought to myself, *What the hell is she talking about? Do I need someone to hold space for me? Like an air hug?* These are serious thoughts I had about what holding space meant. It was so obvious that my spirit and body had not been aligned and caused me to go ungrounded and lost in how I lived my life.

Now, thankfully, I am able to allow others to hold space for me and also hold space for myself. What exactly does this mean? When I am surrounded by others who allow me to share my story, I feel safe to let my emotions flow, whether that means I laugh or cry. Over the years, I've learned that holding space is how another person's energy surrounds me with love and compassion. It does not take my life-force energy from me but helps me to restore my own. For the first time in my entire life, I was starting to become aware of what it means to be truly embodied. A spirit deeply inside my body, docked for life. It's such a blessing to have this type of energetic medicine in my life. At any time, I can reground, bring myself back into my body, fill my own body up with only my own energy, and release anything that is not mine without judgment. It's a powerful practice, which, to be honest, took some time to adjust to because I had been used to giving away my energy to others all the time, not realizing how detrimental it was to my health and how, over time, it literally leads to dis-ease. Now, when I remind myself to hold space for the real deal Jamie, I know I am safe to be fully me there, to cry, yell, dance, sing, and remind myself that everything will be okay. It's the precious moments when I am most present with myself and with life itself that I can trust the path before me, even if I cannot fully see it—literally and figuratively. The irony in losing my sight is that I have been on a journey of learning how to trust the unknown. This path is leading me to live from my highest potential and help others find their way to their own higher good. I would have never in a million years thought that was possible the day I was diagnosed. The Spot had a point. The plot was not lost. I was living my story, and more importantly, choosing the story I wished to tell. While I might have lost complete central vision in my left eye, I could still see light from my right. Regardless of what vision remains for me, I know I have agency in how I respond to this situation now, or anything else that shows up in my life. I did not need to be a martyr. I could and would find my way through this with gratitude and even joy.

Staying with the theme of music and grounding, the song "Joy" by For King and Country brought up a lot of questions for me. The main one was, What the hell brings me joy? Of course, I could say my family, children, and friends, but those are a given. It was really hard for me to answer that question, until I took the time to really ground myself and breathe. As I pondered this question I recalled a conversation I'd had with my friend Bonnie. She reminded me there are two types of joy: Hard Joy and Easy Joy. Hard Joy can be having children, getting and being married, working at a job you love, hanging with your friends, buying a house, etc. Easy Joy can be the smell of your favorite flower, the sound of a baby laughing, seeing the brilliant colors on the trees in the fall, the taste of your favorite dessert, a passionate kiss, etc. Knowing we have Hard Joy and Easy Joy was great, and yet I felt like there was something missing. So, while I was taking the time to ground myself, I heard my spirit ask, "What brings your soul joy, Jamie?" When really thinking about this question I found it hard to answer. I wasn't alone, because I surveyed a few of my friends and asked them the same question. Out of those friends that I asked, a large majority of them couldn't tell me what brought their soul joy. So, again while taking the time to ground myself, I finally connected the dots and it hit me like a freight train. Music brings my soul joy. Not only does it help me ground, but it lights me up with happiness, light, and peace all at the same time. Pure soul joy is the one thing you can always rely on to lift you out of a shitty mood or bad situation. We all have some sort of pure soul joy—we just have to ask ourselves what that is and listen to what our soul relays back to us.

The day I chose joy in dealing with my visual impairment was the day I knew I could help others find joy within themselves, and the peace of mind that comes with it.

***

As I was starting to hold space for others and allow others to hold space for me, I felt my mind and spirit open to a new vocabulary of words, meanings, and modalities that would ultimately help me heal myself.

I have mentioned a few modalities that I have been fortunate to experience; craniosacral therapy, acupuncture, and various forms of energy healing to name a few. One of those energy healing modalities was when I visited a practitioner who specialized in qigong (chi gong). He was a self-described medical chi gong master. He was a very cool guy who, based on my first impression, sounded like he knew what he was talking about and also came highly recommended. When I arrived for my appointment with him, I honestly didn't know what to expect, being that I had no real idea what the hell qigong actually was. As he explained it to me, I knew that this modality involved using exercises to optimize energy within the body, mind, and spirit, with the goal of improving and maintaining health and well-being. Qigong has both psychological and physical components and involves the regulation of the mind, breath, and body's movement and posture. So, as I sat there ready for this medical qigong master to heal me and hopefully help restore my eyesight, I realized that the next words that came out of his mouth had me saying to myself, *WTF!* As I was sitting there blindfolded, which is funny in itself, and trying to clear my mind while he led me through a guided meditation, I heard him say to me, "I am going to heal you today. You will leave here and be able to see!" I internally belly laughed because that comment triggered a memory in me. While I was a college freshman, I met a guy at a nightclub in Hollywood, and his pick up line to me was, "I can make you cum in three minutes or less." With a challenging look on my face, my response to him was, "Bring it on, baby!" Needless to say, he did not succeed in his declaration, unfortunately. So when the medical qigong master stated he was going to heal me by the end of our two hours together, I instantly retreated into my head and dug my heels in, acting like a spoiled child not wanting to leave the playground. Just like with the guy at the nightclub, I was disappointed I didn't get what I was promised.

Looking back now, I can see what might have been askew in those two scenarios as well as many others in my life. Being grounded is self-healing 101. Now that I was traveling down the self-love, spirituality, and healing road, the words *grounding, auras, chakras, life-source energy, meditation sanctuary, visualization techniques,* as well as ways and words to help me help myself, appeared. I decided I needed to start from the beginning and with the simplest and quickest way for me to heal myself. I had to surrender to releasing my fears and controlling tendencies by learning how to ground myself. There are many ways to achieve a feeling of grounding. I have come to learn that the best way for me to ground myself is to stand with my bare feet planted on the ground, preferably outside, and imagine roots pouring out from the bottoms of my feet into the earth and anchoring me into place. This is all happening while I am letting Mother Earth take the fear, resistance, self-loathing, pity, and sadness that is no longer serving me and my higher good. Releasing these feelings into the earth gives me a sense of feeling more peaceful and centered. While doing the grounding work I also take three deep breaths. This helps in reminding me to be present and just let that shit go! The beauty of grounding into the earth is that not only do you get to release those feelings and negative energy that is not serving you in becoming your best self, grounding gives you the gift of receiving healing energy from Mother Earth. This type of grounding can help with reducing inflammation, anxiety, depression, and other ailments that people might have. The book, *Earthing,* by Clinton Ober and Steven T. Sinatra, explains this perfectly and with scientific studies to back up the effects of how being grounded can help us to heal ourselves.

Of course, there are days when the weather isn't cooperating and going outside to ground into the earth isn't an option. I have found other ways to get myself grounded and find peace within myself. Sometimes my grounding for myself comes in the form of music. Music has been such an integral part of my healing that until recently, I didn't realize how much listening to music allowed me to let go of unwanted or unnecessary feelings, allowing me to be present and breathe. I can now tell when I am not grounded, when I don't pay attention and get a little cocky and tend to trip over my own feet, like one day when I stepped off of the porch from our house and missed a step, falling forward and landing on my knees after rolling my ankle. I know what you are saying: "Well, shit, girl, remember you are blind!" I know all of that and sensed where I was stepping to and instead of feeling for the step, I just went for it. I was in my head and not grounded. It's a constant battle to remind myself to be grounded, and I am getting better at it every day.

***

As mentioned earlier, music is a grounding source for me. I have found that any type of music can be grounding for myself and maybe others. Especially when it is live music.

I tested this theory out when I went to see the Foo Fighters live in concert in Tahoe. It was in an outdoor venue, and I felt transported to an alternate universe where I felt normal and free. I still had my cane and needed help navigating the space and people around me, but fuck, was it rad to be there. My BFF Maria was there with me and was my eyes for the evening. She and I had tickets for the grassy area near the stage and were able to snag a spot near the front of the stage. We met a couple with their young adult children. We became fast friends, because everywhere I go I find a connection with those around me because I am exactly where I am supposed to be. Needless to say, the concert was amazing. I "rocked out with my cane out"! For three hours I didn't move from my spot near the stage; I sang, danced, raised my hands into the air like I just didn't care, and felt so incredibly grounded it was surreal. I realized, too, that I'd manifested this experience. I'd visualized myself singing and dancing at a music festival or concert when I was wearing my big-ass headphones, without realizing it was grounding myself at the same time.

Although being at a live rock concert is an experience everyone should have, I know it might not be for everyone. Whatever type of music suits you the best to help you ground is perfect for you.

As I was learning one of the many ways to ground myself and stay present during this time in my life, it dawned on me while I was standing in the crowd of Foo Fighters fans that I was the new and improved Jamie. Meaning, although I have this disability and need a cane to help me navigate my physical movements, I didn't need my sight to hear and feel the music. I put myself in the middle of that crowd knowing I couldn't clearly see Dave Grohl and the other members of the band perform. But ironically, I felt seen by them and the others surrounding me on that lawn in front of the stage. I think the a-ha moment for me at that time was that all along I have wanted to just be seen. Not as a gal who is rocking out with her cane out and is blind but as a gal who is living her best life! I was still working on navigating all that I see within the veil, and myself, too. This meant I would have to have a hard conversation with myself and really listen to what my spirit was trying to tell me. I know she sees me and has been showing me through the veil what everything I have been shown means. There is a method to this madness; I just have to open my eyes to see it.

CHAPTER 20

IN YOUR EYES

IN THE EIGHTIES, THE ICONIC movie, *Say Anything*, was one I will never forget. The scene where Lloyd is holding the giant radio over his head while standing outside Diane's window, with the song "In Your Eyes" by Peter Gabriel blaring out for Diane to hear the words and know he loves her and sees her, is iconic. But the song is what really speaks to me. What is in my eyes? Well... there is so much I see that it becomes a bit overwhelming at times. I continue to decipher what it is I am actually seeing and how best to explain it.

To fully relay what I see, I want to take a step back to when I returned home from my stint at the Stanford weight-loss camp aka my five-day hospital stay. As I mentioned earlier, upon returning home from my stay at Stanford I went from having at least 40 percent clear eyesight to still having some sight but with the surprise of the veil.

When this first happened to me, the best way I could describe it to others was for them to imagine pulling a sweater over their head and looking through the threads. Another description I would give was for them to imagine pressing their face into a screen door and trying to focus on what was behind the screen. Once I got that explanation down, the veil morphed to something else. It then showed up as if I was looking at a static television; I could see the static and kind of make out what was behind the static but not clearly, which was super frustrating and a complete mind fuck. It was almost like someone had put some sort of adhesive over both of my eyes so that no matter if my eyes were opened or closed the veil was always there.

At one point a trusted friend suggested I might be looking into other dimensions. This was suggested because the veil had now morphed into something new. I felt like the morphing of the veil was happening slowly and too fast at the same time. From the end of June 2021 to the end of August 2021 I was looking at another phase of the veil. The third rendition of the veil was as if I was looking at the stars and galaxy in constant motion. So, when the doctors at Stanford asked me to focus on one spot in the box while my chin rested on the plastic notch, it was a big challenge, considering that the veil was in constant motion, kind of like looking through a galactic kaleidoscope.

Once the galaxy showed up things got even weirder. Especially at night. I would get cocky and turn off the lights in the living room and travel to my bedroom. It looked like I was in a laser light show. There were multiple colors shooting across my visual field, and I raised my hands high in the air like I was at a rave. It made me laugh, and as we all know by now, humor and laughter were my coping mechanism. I would sit in my bedroom chair and take a few deep breaths, trying to calm down and figure out what the hell was going on with me. As I sat there, I would close my eyes, and through the veil I was shown bubbles, similar to what I imagine it would feel like to sit in a glass of carbonated water. There were bubbles floating up all around me. Was I getting put through the spiritual wash cycles? What was even trippier was what happened in those moments. If you have ever been hypnotized you will understand.

It was like the Universe told my brain and body to rest while my subconscious and spirit were wide awake. I was conscious of what was happening to me but couldn't pull myself out of it. My body would relax and my chin would drop down to my chest. After a few moments, my head would rise and it was as if I was listening to someone or something telling me a story. My face would have expressions on it that I was aware of but I couldn't tell you what it was that was being said or shown. At times I would burst out laughing or cry an ugly cry. Most of these evening interactions lasted for only minutes. My chin would drop back down to my chest and I would essentially wake up and be back to my normal visually impaired self. The veil was still showing me galaxies and laser light shows until mid-September 2021, when things got really strange.

I was seeing some pretty weird shit. Right before I was invited to meet with the Rose Girls, the veil had a new surprise for me. I was now looking through a blank Etch-A-Sketch with lava lamp liquid, stardust, and little black fibers floating around; the veil had morphed again. By now, though, we were way past the galaxy and lasers. Shit was getting real, and the universe wanted me to pay attention. So, this is when those little black fibers created the images of boobs. So many shapes and sizes. It was a message I didn't quite understand and another trusted friend suggested it was a message from the Divine Feminine. Honestly, I didn't know a Divine Feminine existed. But from what I understand now, the Divine Feminine is a spiritual concept that has recently gained greater attention. It refers to the feminine energy in all of us, regardless of gender identity. The meaning of the Divine Feminine represents the qualities of nurturing, compassion, and intuition generally associated with femininity.

So the question then presented itself: Was I living in the feminine energy now compared to what I had been living in before The Spot appeared, the masculine energy? That is exactly what it felt like, and obviously the Universe wanted to make it perfectly clear I needed to shift my perspective on the way I was living my life. I was moving through my life in an intense masculine energy: direct, aggressive, and action-oriented with a focus on achievement.

At the gathering of women in mid-September 2021, I was seeing the boobs in my visual field and, without any prodding on my part, the animal eyes started flooding my visual field. It was like a constant movie or slideshow running non-stop. These eyes of mainly lions, tigers, owls, and eagles would continuously look at me throughout the day and night. It didn't matter if my eyes were opened or closed; these eyes made their presence known. I didn't know at the time what the hell these specific eyes were doing, staring at me in a very passive way. They were never scary or predatory. I realize now they were telling me to be brave, let go of my fear, look all around me, and let go of doubt so I could soar into the next phase of life's adventures.

I found comfort in seeing these specific eyes every day and was secretly excited to see the eyes of other animals show up as well. At one point I thought to myself, *In a past life was I on Noah's Ark?* Seeing these eyes gave me a sense of peace, and it was as if the spirits of these animals were letting me know that they could see me, too, and that I would be okay.

But of course, the minute I got comfortable with this form of the veil, it decided to morph one more time. My animal eyes were still showing up but now they had some friends with them. Those friends were the eyes of what looked like humans. Again, some of these eyes were colored but most of them were like looking at a sketch of eyes in black, white, and gray. Some of the eyes were closed and I only saw the eyelashes. The eyes varied in size—some were large, and it was like the spirit was standing right in front of me and staring me in the face, while others were smaller and seemed to be far away. Most of the time they were very passive and loving. Periodically, though, a set of eyes would show up with a surprised expression or they would look at me with an inquisitive expression. Honestly, the whole thing was super magical and trippy.

I got the sense that the eyes I was now seeing were all different spirits checking me out. I wondered if in some way I was connected to each of these spirits, whether we were connected in this life or a past life. What I have now come to understand is that these eyes were sending me a strong message, one I had previously refused to acknowledge: I am seen. I am seen in spite of wearing the mask that I have always worn

All of these eyes have been a part of my life now for three years. I only feel love and compassion for all of them. This is another part of the surrender I need to embrace. They are trying to tell me something, and I know that when I get quiet and listen, they will talk to me. The surrender part of this facet of my journey is to trust in the process of what is and has happened to me to get me to where I am today, then to believe in the possibilities that are and will be presented to me. This will ultimately allow me to embrace and move forward in my life's journey, so I can accept this path I am now on—this path that is full of love, protection, curiosity, intuition, and the ability to help others on their life journey, too.

Since starting to write this book, the eyes have been a constant, and I have gotten used to them. Because the Universe has a sense of humor, it thought it would be fun to show me numbers and faces of people I do know and others I don't know. I guess the message that I am to surrender to, is that yes, I am looking into other dimensions to see more than just with my eyes.

***

I know there is more that I am to see and not just with my eyes—I am seeing with more intuitive and loving eyes or vision. I have also found that when I am able to sit and be present more than just eyes show up. For instance, I was at a sound healing, which consisted of my friend Jillian playing her crystal singing bowls. The sounds she created with these bowls was, for lack of a better word, magical! After she led us through a grounding meditation, she began playing the bowls, and they literally sang to me. The sounds enabled me to go into a deep meditation where I asked myself what I needed to see and work through. What trauma and anger had I not dealt with since losing my eyesight? What I heard in my mind's eye was that I needed to let go and surrender to what happened to me during those months of April to June 2021. I was shown a vision. I saw myself laying in the hospital bed at our local hospital before being transferred to Stanford. I was asleep, and there were four other figures in the room with me. The first of the four figures to speak to me was one of my spirit guides. His name is Ian, and he was wearing scrubs and a white coat, looking very much like a doctor. He told me he was with me during my stays at the hospital and that he was helping to guide the doctors and nurses in taking care of me and getting me to where I needed to go, hence my luck in getting a room at Stanford via my friend Lynette's help. The next figure in the room to speak up was another one of my spirit guides. His name is Sebastian, but I call him Seb. He is a light-colored Black man with beautiful braided hair, and he let me know he is my personal DJ. He brings me music, as he knows that is what brings me pure soul joy and will also help me heal and flow with the light energy. The other two figures that were in the room with me evoked so much emotion. As I mentioned, this scene had me sleeping in the hospital bed. I realized I was watching myself; it was surreal. In this vision I looked to the opposing wall and saw the third figure standing there in the dark. She looked like me, but gray and gaunt; clearly drained and exhausted. I instantly knew she was my shadow self. The fourth figure was standing at the side of my bed. She was leaning over my sleeping body and was gently holding my face in both of her hands. She was speaking to me and saying, "Jamie, listen, you are going to go blind. It is going to be really hard for you and your life is going to change. The change will be what is necessary for you to transition and move forward. You will have experiences and challenges that only you can endure. Know that what is happening is not happening to you but for you. Your shadow side has been wreaking havoc on you and she is tapping out because you don't need her—you don't need the fear and anxiety and self-doubt that has been your main *modus operandi* for most of your life. You are light. You are energy that flows. You have the ability to help others, to teach others. Your gut will heal; the right doctors and nurses are lined up to help you with all of that. Your eyes, though, that is going to take some time. You were always looking for the next thing, the love you felt you needed but didn't deserve, the bigger home, better car, etc. But, sweet Jamie, all you had to do was see what was inside of you all along. You have so much light and love glowing inside you and now all around you, it pulses, and once you surrender to this you will see what you were always supposed to see. Your daughter said it to you when she was three years old. You were videotaping her playing with her brother in the house and she would say to you, 'Mom, I see me!' She wanted to see her light and how beautiful she was and is. She was showing you how. You also are beautiful and your light is worth seeing. You will heal, Jamie; I am always with you."

This figure leaning over my body was, without a doubt, my spirit. She was wearing a white gown and looked like me. She was glowing with gold all around her. It was so beautiful; I am so grateful and am now seeing what I was meant to see. I see me, I see the beauty around me, I see the love that surrounds me, I see the abundance that is ahead of me and the healing that is in my eyes.

I have been given a fresh piece of paper so that I can write this new story, which will allow my loving river for myself and others to flow into my heart and seep into the rest of my body, creating healing and a knowing that I can finally see me and she is a badass! What I know now is that

I am blind but I can see… and what I see is my ability to surrender and see all that is in front of me.

I have finally arrived at the in-between moments, where I can close my eyes, have fallen in love, and am okay staying there.

ACKNOWLEDGMENTS

THERE AREN'T ENOUGH words to express the amount of gratitude I have for everyone who has witnessed or been a part of this journey with me. Every day I am in awe of the love and support that my family and I have been blessed with and know that without these people in our lives, this book would not have been possible to share with you, the reader.

With that said, thank you for taking the time to read my story. For taking the time to see that even though your story might be different, we are all experiencing our own unique journey. When we are able to share it with at least one person, it has such a profound effect on how we traverse this human experience. Because ultimately, we *are* souls having a human experience, right?

My heart swells with love and gratitude to:

> My family: my husband, Stewart, and my three children, Mackenzie, Hayden, and Grady
>
> My mom, Shirley Minton
>
> My sister, Sara Minton Beken and her husband, Sean Beken
>
> My dad, Jim Ribas
>
> My brother, Michael Ribas

The Mintons, including my aunts and uncles who have loved me since I was in my mom's belly.

The Roth family

Thank you to all of the beautiful souls/friends who held me up when I crumbled, who laughed with me when I needed to breathe, who protected me from any literal falls or weird outfits, for keeping it real and never letting me forget how much I am loved, and for always having my back.

Maria Giannini
Jenny Leamey
Michelle Borgomini
Molly Meyer
Jennifer Vanoli
Rita Pruthi
Kristen Moore
Bonnie Bufkin
Kelly Davidian
Lynn Cordell
Jennifer Olsen
Kori Lukasko
Charlotte Gannoway
John Carmen
Kathleen (Kat) McCrystal
Kristen Kitaji
Raul and Coleen Pantoja
Jen Jacobs Bolger
Jill Sleeper
Carolyn Genacaou
Wendy Reynolds
Allison Mahan Sojka
Sunol Patel

Marilyn Getas Byrne
Jordan Williams
My Minor Mystic posse: Tara Ryan and Morgan Goyette
My soul sisters of the Woo-Woo Book Club:
Venessa Gilbride
Eva Nelson Cole
Shannon Curran Hanley
Jillian Engstrome
Bernadette Renois
My college girlfriends, who knew me and my twenty-two-year-old self best:
Katie Boudreau LaFontaine
Lynnette Quadrini
Ann Danon
Suzie Cardillo
Eileen McIlrath
Barbie Roth
Nadia Phillips
Lynda Purcell
Big thanks for being an early reader of my book:
Venessa Gilbride
Brooke French
Allyson Huntington
Deborah Peyton
Karen Minton
Daniel Minton
Bella Borgomini
Sarah Salee
Merrie Montogourro
Jennifer Allen and the beautiful ladies of the Women's Wisdom Weaving Circle

SHOULD'VE SEEN THAT COMING

My Glam Squad:
  Kristin Toomey
  Amy Bell
  Brittney Richards
  Laura Salazar
The village of family and friends who helped raise me:
  Judy and john Nelson
  Kathy Johnson
  Mike and Gayle Hefner
  Edna and George Perrington
  Theda Trujillo
  Toni Bustos
  Grandma and Grandpa Ribas
  Grandma and Grandpa Hefner
  Grandma and Grandpa Minton
My Fur Angels:
  Coco
  Bodie
  Rocky
  Koda

This story was just an idea swimming in my head without all of the wonderful humans who have helped me get the words onto paper. I am forever in your debt.

Thank you to the Landon Hail Press family:
  Samantha Joy, Founder & Editor in Chief
  Paige Killian, Book Launch Coach
  Megan Tatreau, Book Editor
  Rich Johnson, Book Cover Designer
Holly Payne, Writing Coach... Thank you for getting me started, for your guidance and encouragement.
  Ashley Dodge, Web Designer

The Pitch Club team:
Rebecca Cafiero
Katie Passarello

A big thank you to all of the energy healers and medical professionals who cared for me with compassion, words of encouragement, and "out of the box" treatments. You all played an integral part of my healing journey:

Sarah Nisse
Kristen White
Kristan Roth
Rob Somers
Cindy Purdy
Julia Joy
John Newton
Judie Brown
Jen Weigel
Caroline Myss
Frank Bruni
Dr. Colvert "Covi" Gonzales and the Hattori Vision
    Team
Dr. Kevin Chen
Dr. Tony Pruthi
Dr. Mark Morrow
Dr. Shannon Beres
Dr. Quan Dong Nguyen
Dr. Mark Vierra
Dr. Maki Takashima
Dr. Julie Kenner

Thank you to all of the nurses, MRI and CT technicians, staff, and administrators for being living angels to me when I was feeling alone and vulnerable while I was being cared

for at Stanford Hospital and Byers Eye Care Center and Community Hospital of the Monterey Peninsula/Montage.
Thank you to the volunteers and caring souls of:
The Blind and Visually Impaired Center of
Monterey County
ITN -Monterey County

You can find more information about Jamie and the work she's doing now by following these links:

Website: www.jamieestelleroth.com

Socials: @jamieestelleroth

Email: info@jamieestelleroth.com

ABOUT THE AUTHOR

FOLLOWING A LIFE-ALTERING medical event, the loss of her vision in her early fifties, Jamie Roth has focused on her personal journey of growth and teaching others about spiritual awakening in the face of despair. Her path through this transformative journey has shown itself to be a triumph of resilience and acceptance.

Jamie Roth, a mother of three children who lives in California with her husband, Stewart, spreads the message of finding one's purpose in times of tragedy not only through her debut book, *Should've Seen That Coming,* but by co-hosting the podcast *Minor Mystics* with Tara Ryan.

Jamie's spiritual awakening and personal growth following a tragic medical event have shown just how much of a fighter she is in times of hardship. Although her vision may have been altered, her purpose was not. Jamie is a beacon of hope, of resilience, and of unwavering strength.

Website: www.jamieestelleroth.com
Socials: @jamieestelleroth
Email: info@jamieestelleroth.com

Made in the USA
Las Vegas, NV
07 December 2024

13510686R00134